Dear Ahvi,

Thought you and
bedtime reading -

Now his *strong* ... !!

See you soon,

Lov

John
xxx

Daily Life

A different message

Other poetry books in this series

From Darkness to Life
A Spiritual Journey

In the series
Verses that mean a lot

Growing Up
Coping with Illness and Grief
Choice for Teenagers

BOOK

Beyond Mercy

First published by
PLP Publishings(UK) in 2010

PLP Publishings(UK), PO Box 2150, Buckingham, MK18 1UR

Note to the Reader

This publication does not attempt to dispense or prescribe for or treat medical or psychological problems. If the reader, or other for whom this publication is intended, has significant difficulties in life it is highly recommended that they seek an appropriate medical practitioner.

ISBN 978-0-9555310-6-4

Printed and bound by **Mayfield Press (Oxford) Ltd**

Distributed by
PLP Publishings, PO Box 2150, Buckingham, MK18 1UR

Websites:
www.plppublishings.com
www.audreycoatesworth.com
Email:
audrey.coatesworth@virgin.net

Acknowledgements

To my husband, Peter

For his continued care, support, devotion and love throughout my
long and difficult illness and always keeping faith with me that I
would reach the end of my journey

To Hedy

For the gift of the original Logo

FOREWORD

Medicine has been my profession
In Psychiatry I specialised
I am a wife and mother
My grandchildren are idolised
But
I do not consider myself a poet
Though many verses you will find
Written over several years
From deep within my mind
Why?
No knowledge about the metre
Ottava rima, terzains or Sapphics
And, truthfully, I had never heard
Of iambs or hudibrastics
I read one day there were anapaests
Though I never explored the rest
To find out about spenserians
Would not my time use best
Quatrains or sixains mean nothing
And rime royals have passed me by
My verses have a purpose
To make people laugh or cry
No need of analysis by scholars
I doubt mine will reach their gaze
I have written these messages
To help people walk life's maze
Nothing difficult, nothing fancy
But about times we all may face
They have been written from my heart
Maybe in yours they will find a place

Audrey Coatesworth 2010

► ◄

CONTENTS

A Dreamer

She was young. She had a dream
She was just fourteen
To be a doctor when she grew up
And that is what she's been

She was young. She had a dream
To be a wife and mother
She could work hard to be a doctor
But this depended on another

She was young. She had a dream
She would be well and strong
The other could not help in this
Someone else must come along

She was young she had a dream.
She had two sisters dear
They would never tire of her
And help her through all fear

The first dream became reality
The second, true love she found
The third, is not yet resolved
The fourth, is heaven bound

She was born a dreamer
But to work and suffer too
To strive has been her lifetime
And she still has much to do
If she can, she most surely will
If she can't, at least she's tried
And on the journey many tears
Of joy and sorrow cried

► ◄

A View of Christmas

Christmas has been and gone
And left not the faintest trace
Of religion, or joy and peace
As it never reached my space
Pain came instead of Santa
Bed instead of 'a ball'
And I felt too ill to meet
Or ask anyone to call
Did I miss something special?
The beliefs I don't accept?
The gifts and waste of money
Excessive food that all expect?
No, the only thing I regret
I didn't see the children's faces
With them I didn't play or sing
In one of my favourite places

I hate to see extravagance
As debts build up unseen
I dislike the hypocrisy
And all gluttony is obscene
So, goodbye to my Christmas
And with it take the pain
I missed only what a holiday
Could have given me to gain
One day sense will return
Compassion be of more worth
Those who now ruin health
Will regret their wasted birth
Only themselves, not Christ
Will have to take the blame
Health is the most important goal
For which everyone should aim

▶ ◀

An Example

I write to men everywhere
The world a better place would be
If men shared and cared as much
As my husband has done for me
Illness has walked in my footsteps
Assistance thus was needed
He has had his own busy life
But my calls were always heeded

In times that were dire and drear
Around my shoulder was his arm
He did everything that he could
To keep us fed and warm
No thought, during many years
That the time that was passing by
Was not just mine, but his life too
At my pain I saw him cry

Not knowing what the future held
He watched and helped throughout
With no thought of personal gain
Each day showed not a doubt
Now, I recover, with great thanks
For his patience, love and care
I nearly died, but I couldn't leave
Love wouldn't pay the fare

If all men in this world would listen
Take an example from 'the best'
Work hard, give understanding love
Poverty and wars could have a rest
No money wasted in killing fields
Women would true justice meet
Countries could thrive in peacetime
And children have enough to eat

▶ ◀

<u>Arrogance</u>

I've met people who were arrogant
They thought themselves so clever
They didn't know what they lacked
And would not listen - ever
But people believed their bull-shit
And listened to them speak
They will, one day, tumble
Down from their highest peak

A mistake was never seen as theirs
Blame arrived on other's knee
They would even get some praise
Their foolish acts no one could see
How can it be that arrogance
Can hide truth within its sphere?
The voice, their secret weapon, masks
Ignorance between each ear

Balanced Thinking

If you were to make a picture of a room, its colour and its size
All contents in their place
You would be quick and no surprise
You could imagine, if you wished
How it would look if it was changed
Different curtains, different walls
And the furniture rearranged

If you were to describe in words the same room and get it right
It could take you all the day and
Probably half the night
To describe the exacts colours
The relative sizes to itemise
The shades of light upon the wall
To complete you'd earn a prize

How would you tell others what the room was like with feelings?
Descriptions, hard or soft
Warm or cold are not revealing
The atmosphere of the room
And whether it's liked or hated
Cannot be conveyed with ease as
Few clues are circulated

When decisions must be made, what is your favourite way?
Do you see alternatives in your head?
And then let the best one stay?
Looking at the outcome with
Different scenarios there could be
Put in all the information
And the possible futures see?

Or do you become lost, inner words go round and round
And the decision can't be made
No compromise to be found
The thoughts get stuck in circles
Part of you thinks it knows the best

It is reasoning without vision
So it cannot know the rest

Maybe you make an instant choice based on feelings at the time
And then regret what you have done
When you find that it's not fine
It doesn't fit what you want
When or where it could be needed
But you just went 'with your heart'
And your mind, simply, was not heeded

When traumas affect our young minds, when still immature
One of these modes takes over
A good job it will then ensure
At least that is what it thinks
But it has not got it straight
As all these modes of thinking need
To have about equal weight

We need to have some vision, we need to reason through
We need to feel right from wrong
Together these modes aid you
To follow the path that we should tread
To be kind, fulfilled, content
Our decisions must be balanced
Then our lives will be 'as meant'

No-one would hurt another as they would see and feel the pain

No-one would be arrogant, learn some words have naught to gain

No-one would take what isn't theirs instead offer a helping hand

Everyone could learn to value the place where others stand

▶ ◀

Being Dependent

I need you to be around to be my hands and feet
To be well is my intention. All efforts to that end meet

Yet on and on and on it goes. Tribulation without end
I despair, I cry, am angry, for myself I want to fend

I am belittled by this struggle. My emotions all lay bare
My wellbeing is dependant on your willingness to care

An end to all reliance, independence is my goal
To do and be and live again, myself once more to own

I have no energy left within me sufficient for that task
Patience, please stay longer with us both, that's all I ask

Long, hard times make demands which make us lose the sight
Of how we lived in the past before this endless night

But Hope lives on despite all, with Courage, a friend to treasure
Resilience we have dearly learned and effort beyond all measure

One day we shall laugh again, of that I am quite sure
I survive to be with you and through all love will endure

Blinkered by Belief

Your smile lights up your face
As though the sun shines through
For others' words, for others' deeds
For the same, what must I do?
With them you look so pretty
But then your face turns old
Why is that? I ask myself
Is it the scowl? The look so cold?

I used to want to see that light
When I came through the door
It never seemed to happen
So I keep my dream no more
For you, I am a sorrow
I listened, you said that word
Sometimes I am glad I know
Then wish I had not heard

You believe that god created
All creatures great and small
If so, he made me as I am
My body, mind and all
I cannot believe as you do
It is not something you can change
I let my mind travel
Over all things it can range

Religion I can not tolerate
You live with your belief
When your god asks his questions
Will you tell him of your grief?
I'd love to know his answer
Would he with you agree?
Or would he say you were foolish
When you were so blind to me?

►◄

Choosing an Epitaph

If I could choose my epitaph, somewhere it would contain
The few words, 'She was kind' and
Above all, 'She hated pain'

Kindness is worth more than gold, than riches, however great
Any achievement I may gain
No higher value will create

I speak with sharpened tongue against cruelty or selfish greed
I doubt my time is quite enough
For my message to succeed

To stand the ground for another who cannot fight their right
Abhorrence against injustice
Will fire my inner might

All who hurt young children, or innocents, for evil's sake
Will know I shall never rest
They have made a big mistake

When I abide on higher realm look down on actions dire
I shall intercede for no mercy
They shall meet eternal fire

No mellowing in my old age, no forgiveness for hurt inflicted
As, out of sadistic greed and lust
They have their fate directed

Kindness would never reach them. That belief will live for ever
They shall reap what they have sown
With no time to repent at leisure

Convalescence

I wasn't allowed to die, though dying holds no fear
But I can't seem to live
My body holds me to ransom still so much pain to feel
What more must I give?

Joy has now departed. Despair and sadness reign
What I need is laughter
But, as yet, inside my head, that is nowhere to be found
I'm told it 'comes after'

Recovery is my final goal, convalescence an easy word
But how can I still cope?
Exhaustion's extra problems just add to the endless strife
I try very hard to hope

When I can live a life again, will everything begin anew
And be different from the last?
Must I another mountain climb? Ford unmapped rivers deep
Before I leave the past?

I do not know the answers yet, one day maybe shall find
The future way ahead
Till then I must rest a lot, keep sane with reason's balm
And watch TV from my bed

Conversations at the Nursery

'Why are you here every day?'

'Because mummy is unkind
She shouts and has been known
To hit my bare behind
I was crying, I had tummy ache
I couldn't bear the griping pain
Finger marks stayed there
She hit me, then hit again
Someone saw her do it
And reported her and soon
I had to be here all the time
I see her most days, about noon'

'My Mummy is not like that at all
She is very sweet and gentle
She is so intelligent that looking
After me just drives her mental
I heard her say she needs something
Called 'rational adult talk'
So she just leaves me every day
Then drives happily to her work
Maybe there she is clever
But with me she's not too bright
She doesn't know how to stop me
When I test her through the night'

'I do not have a daddy
My Mother had me on her own
She is kind and loves me
But needs money for a phone
To ring granny and her best friend
And my aunties Sue and Lizzy
They all say they love me
I see so many. My head is dizzy
I nearly know their faces

But I'm not sure where I live
As Mother will just take me
And to someone different give'

'I come from a wealthy family
Mummy thinks I am a guest
She doesn't know about child rearing
'It's for those who must know best'
She reads books about psychology
And Feng Shui to name a few
I don't think she knows me at all
But her mother she never knew
She doesn't want a nanny
As she would clutter up the house
But if I could just stay at home
I would be quiet as any mouse'

'I wish I was at home now
Where I could quietly sleep
There is just too much noise
And wide awake I keep
I have such a lovely bedroom
With a mobile made of wood
I have toys piled around my cot
And my soft teddy feels so good'

'My head aches with my cold
My chest hurts when I cough
Why can't I just stay at home?
I am little and life's so tough'

'I don't know why I was born
A mother I will never be
Unless I can care for my baby
So she won't have a life like me
I don't recognise where I am
What if they forget to call
To pick me up to take me home?
I can't find the way at all'

'If a career is so important
Status, clothes and a new car
Why did my mother have me?
I'd be better not born, by far'

'I took my first step today and
I said 'Mama', my first word
But the lady did not respond
As if she had never heard'

'That's because she is not your Mama
And has heard it all before
Others have taken 'first steps'
There's no excitement any more'

'I'm sad my Mummy missed it
But why should I try to wait?
Until she comes and collects me
She went out through that gate'

Many others shared their troubles
Talked of dark, missed days of love
Discussed the deep black hole within
Some learned to rise above
They had to cope by switching off
Their emotions one by one
Until, finally, like little robots
Pain and feeling had now gone

The emotions of a few remained
Some were angry, some were sad
They were confused as they knew
Most parents were not bad

The children in the nursery
Shared their thoughts - in vain
No one knew what was going on
In each little person's brain

Longing, lonely, lost and sad
Felt in their body and their mind
A loving mother to a tiny child is
More important than all mankind

That role is usually taken on
With great pride and glowing joy
But other 'needs' can soon appear
To usurp a baby girl or boy

So, they presented smiling faces
As they knew that was the way
Hoped people would remain kind
As they learned they had to stay

'Such a good child'

'Oh so sweet'

'She's quiet as a mouse
But, of course, you understand
We want a bigger house'

'I miss being with her, naturally'

'Yes, I am sure I'm doing right'

'The only problem that we've got
She will not sleep at night'

Denied

I would love to swim in water
By sunny beach or indoor pool
But I am sitting fully dressed
In the shade. At least I'm cool
I would love to walk along a track
Over moors, through leafy glens
But I just watch the videos
Through someone else's lens

My lot to watch, observe and dream
All the things I cannot do
I must compensate, accept, or else
I'd regret my whole life through
What a waste that would be
But I wish I had been born
Without so many ideas and dreams
Then I would not be forlorn

My mind used to shout and scream
Then it was strange. One day
I realised that all my time
Was of value in some way
I love to see others play
Swimming, dancing, having fun
One day, I keep my hope alive
I shall, in sunlight, run

Most know not this awful feeling
And for that I'm very glad
Knowing the same all would learn
The life some others had
Would it make a difference if
All were aware within their mind
That life can be so difficult?

~

Would people be more kind?

► ◄

Destitution

'Is there kindness anywhere?'

Each to the other said

*'Young girls, you look hungry
Please, share my piece of bread'*

'Is there courage anywhere? Will no one for us speak?'

*'The world has many cowards
Who gain energy from the weak'*

'Is the world just full of tears like ours?'

The young girls cried

*'Sorrow is not something
Which those people ever tried'*

'We believe within our hearts, one day we shall be free
To walk amidst scented flowers and just sit beneath a tree
Nothing special, nothing grand, we require not that at all
But we want to be allowed to run, skip and never fall
No work, no hurt, not one tear, even dreams will have no pain
We shall leave, and walk away and never come back again'

*'You look for a miracle
But that will not come true'*

'In that case, we have no choice. Somehow, we must get through'

*'You have kindness. You are brave
Despite nothing in your hand
You are a place of goodness
Used by guiding stars to land'*

Differences

All is expected no leeway allowed
No error forgiven all words avowed
Nothing forgotten rules only apply
To the one person who really will try
Others can shirk the rules become riven

'They must be tired'

So all is forgiven

No lapses are noticed, how silly to think
They can sit down. I wash pots in the sink
I'm blunt. They're honest. I'm rude. They're clear
You're cruel, and strict, then I shed a tear

**'Why can't you behave?
Like everyone else?'
Stop blubbering will you?
Then maybe talk sense'**

Why am I different?
Why can you not see? I am not bad or ungrateful?
Do you not love me?
Others don't help. Others make a mess
I help you to clean

But

You never say 'Yes'

▶ ◀

Different Destination

How many hours can I be
In hell and still survive?
I thought that place was for
The dead, not those alive
For the bad, not the good
The cruel, not the kind
Maybe I don't understand
But, what reason do I find?
I cope with pain bravely
And endure what I must feel?
This is surely part of hell
I was given a roughest deal

I never willingly hurt another
My nature is to care
Yet I have been given pain
More than anyone could bear
I have journeyed into hell
So now I know its measure
If I were one of the bad
I'd change, and not at leisure
I'd soon learn different values
Never cause another pain
I'd alter my destination and
Board a very different train

Different Scenarios

Scenario 1

'Where's the vodka?
Where's the gin?
Just a drop and then
Oh God!
Must the day begin?
It's the school holidays
Children in the way
Just let me get my glass
I can't cope another day
I can't even think about
The effort I must make
Why did I really bother
This day off work to take?'

*'Don't be so pathetic
Put all drink down the sink
Reassess your priorities
And use your mind to think
Children are more important
Than any 'work' can be
Just alter your perspective
And let your heart be free
Your child, your companion
Can become your closest friend
But only if you allow yourself
Time with that child to spend'*

►◄

Scenario 2

'Hurrah! No school today and we can have some fun
It is fine, get ready, the picnic's nearly done
I just love the holidays, time with you to share
We can go to the park and play without a care
We can ask your friends to tea and days together we'll enjoy
No time could be better spent than with you my girl and boy'

~

'Which Mum is happier?'

'Which one do you think?
One who sees motherhood as mere drudgery at a sink?
Or one who welcomes every day
Who shares time without strife
To those who didn't ask, but to whom she gave a life?'

'Why did one bother?
I am tempted that question to raise
Instead of enjoying precious days
She prefers to live life 'in a haze'

Personally, it is my opinion that you get back what you give
Selfishness can only create a negative way to live
Children who are cherished, whose mothers give time and care
Will find an inner strength that with others they can share
But those who feel a nuisance who escaped a 'priority' list
May well ignore a future bond
As
None can regain the time they missed

▶ ◀

Different Times

Maybe you never knew me
You first learned my name
When we were very young
Times were not the same
We counted many, not a few
Who lived within our door
Plenty food for everyone
And those who wanted more
Kindness and companionship
Care, laughter, love and fun
Yes, I can remember all that
A life of summer and of sun

Maybe you never knew me
There was only cold and frost
Winter came, and winter stayed
Then the fog and I was lost
No walks amid the heather
No laughter by the sea
Icicles on roof and gutter
That was all that I could see
Mountains and streams only
In imagination played a part
In a life of daily grind
With my young broken heart

Different Viewpoints

Someone calls but no one hears
A favour asked, request refused
But if something is ever needed
My name can then be used

'Can you do this, can you do that?
It won't take you very long
How good it is to have you
I'm glad that you are strong'

No one notices exhaustion
From endless sleepless nights
To expect constant effort
Is classed as 'normal rights'

Some people are oblivious
Others, quite simply, do not care
That there are many people
Of life's fun have not a share

Does it matter in the order
Of the vast universe around?
That while one runs a marathon
Someone else crawls on the ground?

Looking down on this world
What message would we give?
What judgment could be made?
Of the ways in which we live

▶ ◀

Disapproval

Of my actions, my beliefs
You may disapprove outright
Without me who would care?
And keep **you** in their sight

What I believe and think
They are none of your concern
I am what you see and hear
But that you never learn

Religion to me is nothing
Hot air, but not God's word
You believe what you are told
It's as if I am not heard

I believe in an afterlife when
For ourselves we must account
Our actions and our motives
Our memories are the fount

Nothing is wiped away
The traces that are made
In preceding years is when
Eternal destiny is laid

So disapprove all you can
Close your mind if you will
But you will answer at the gate
And pay at heaven's till

If you are happy that is fine
No problem held for you
But, leave me out of your design
I'll find my own way through

► ◄

Discovering Truth

All the days of my life
I have loved to be alive
Tried to make the very best
When winds and storms did rive
When nothing was left but torment
I still lived through each day
But one moment it was too much
Somehow, I couldn't stay

Oh this plane all was pain
A different path I had to take
It was never of my choice
And no decision did I make
It was the way to heaven's gate
I, with shock, then heard

'It is not time for you to stay
Go back, and heed my word'

I was not given an option
But the way was black as night
Who took me there was silent
I was not given any light
Everyone must one day die
Where you go, none can pretend
Too late to be kind when at the gate
No advance letter can you send

No one can ever tell a lie
Or put their record straight
I have visited, heard the truth
Listen carefully, for all just wait
No bartering, no pleasing words
Will find mercy or hear a plea
All are unheeded at that gate
But, the way for all is free

▶ ◀

Doubt

Just what colours I would like
I was sure that you would know
But if you and I think differently
That is really quite a blow

I gained knowledge on my way
I thought what I learned was right
But now I ponder 'is that so'?
When awake throughout the night

Has my effort all been wasted?
These long and trying years
Will the fruits of all endeavours
Only lead to bitter tears?

How can I begin to understand
The wherefores and the why's?
I have studied and I've analysed
The information before my eyes

But now, I have so many doubts
I have thought and thought again
My confidence has been shaken
Will it all have been in vain?

I must just wait with patience
And think, then think some more
If I am meant to know the tune
Please give me the proper score

Effects of Pain

Pain, like a giant siphon
Drains energy away
Enthusiasm cannot live
To greet another day
Wilting like a flower
In a summer's blight
Crumbling in the aftermath
Of another sleepless night
Surely it must all end
Everything has a limit
Removing any pleasure
Does pain have any merit?
Does it teach a lesson?
Endurance?
Patience strong?
Or does it simply mean
Each day seems much too long
Minutes pass like hours
The seconds drag slowly by
My advice, don't grit your teeth
Just give in
And cry

Exhaustion

Have you ever been so tired
That you can hardly think?
Your head starts to ache
And you just want to sink
Into bed with weariness
Attention hard to keep
Limbs weak with fatigue and
You just long to sleep

Snappy - if a question asked?
Too much effort to answer back
The needs of others, even dear
Are ignored. They feel the lack
You argue and do not smile
That change exhaustion brings
Sometimes harsh words are spoken
As the heart no longer sings

Sleep, that blesséd function
To access we really try
So the energy can be restored
To be the self that doesn't cry
Oh! The pleasures of many hours
Of oblivious, true respite
With pleasant dreams that refresh
Until the new day's light

All the chores are left behind
As closed eyes cannot see
Just to sleep, such sweet relief
Nothing now can trouble me
I shall wake refreshed and soon
Be my normal self once more
Understand and let me rest
Then I shall be 'perfect' - as before

► ◄

Facing Life

In the order of the universe
Just a mere speck am I
Yet, pain finds me as its target
I always wonder, 'Why?'
Everything spoiled, no respite
As one heals or disappears
Another comes to affect me
I am made to carry fears

How did I become so obvious?
Normal, in most respects
But pain trails my footsteps
What will happen next?
It has never been the victor
I shall always fight and win
Meet every day with courage
And try to wear a grin

Being miserable doesn't help
Puts a cloud on those I love
They are not responsible
But, I'm angry with those above
I have not been given any time
To enjoy, to laugh or play
When I find the end to pain
It will be **the** most special day

► ◄

Faded Dreams

Shall I stop making dreams?
Projects put to rest?
Disappointment is depressing
So, this strategy may be best
All my life, through much pain
In dire times, not a few
I have planned within my head
Lots of things that I would do
It has always served me well
Distraction through each storm
They were always full of interest
Made me feel life was 'the norm'
If health greeted me at dawn
And I recovered strength
Had enough breath to meet the day
In my mind I'd find a wealth
Of ideas, waiting like open doors
To the order of things to be
But recently those have faded
They seem not to fit with me
I have been patient, as a shepherd
Who sits to watch his sheep
Letting each day go slowly by
And many nights had little sleep
Yet now, my energy fails me when
Extra load lands on my back
Even a camel would falter with
Added straw put in its pack
I always planned a busy life
For a future time, when well
Has it all proved wasted effort?
Who knows?
Just time will tell

►◄

Fading Slowly

Little contact, breathing fast
Her lips a shade of blue
I feared she would be gone by now
Taken by the flu
No food and little fluid
She cannot last this way
Yet she weakly rallies
To meet another day
What keeps this old spirit
Holding on upon this plane?
To other eyes just misery
With nothing left to gain
We cannot know the reason
For the extended length
Her journey was a marathon
Of will and earthly strength
Does our love keep her here?
She never liked a parting
Is she in a queue somewhere?
With no choice
Just waiting?
These questions I ponder
As I sit many bedside hours
Already, with the grief of loss
I see her fading like the flowers
Many tears have been shed and
Many months have passed
Since her present mind was gone
Old memories all that last
One day, in heaven
She will tell me if the vigil was in vain
Or whether
A loving presence helped her
Through her passing's pain

► ◄

False Beliefs

As I was walking out one day, I saw a man at prayer
Kneeling under an oak tree. He was totally unaware
That nearby a little child was crying
Calling out

'Someone, please help me'

His pitiful, mournful shout

As I was walking out one day, I heard a sudden noise
Bells from a gold domed church pealed out with single voice
As the people all filed out they put coins upon a tray
A child sat in the gutter

'I have eaten naught today'

As I was walking out one day, a cavalcade drove past
Decision makers of the world going to a rich repast
I followed through the same route, shacks lined the streets ahead
Children in abject poverty
For them - just scraps of bread

As I was walking out one day, I saw two girls at play
I watched their kindness to a child as they passed her way
They noticed her and stopped, crippled, she could not walk
They held her hands and sang to her
Though she could not talk

They were poor. It appeared they had nothing they could give
With compassion, care and love they chose their lives to live
Many would revile them for their poverty and lowly state
But when they reach heaven's door
They will not have to wait

'Come in, you are very welcome'

The girls would hear one day,

But

'What happened to that child?
While you wasted time to pray'

'The hunger of the poor
We felt as you past you sped'

'A golden dome is pretty, but
It does not need some bread'

'Down that corridor you must go,
The gate will not let you through
It is not my choice but your own
You had freedom what to do
You were blind
You were deaf
Your house was built on sand
The foundations were faulty
Your destiny was in your hand'

'I gave prayers to God daily'

'I worshipped at his knee'

'Whatever you did, it doesn't show here
Your name I cannot see'

'But I ...'

'Those children had no learning
Yet within their heart and mind
They felt the need of another
They were simply, very kind'

Family Ties

'Hello, it's so nice to see you'

Kisses, lightly on each face

'Come in and have a cup of tea
Yes, many changes to this place
I have been so busy
Life seems to just pass by
I would have called to see you
But no time'

Said, with a sigh

'I have been the same as you
We could think we do not care
But there is a bond that comes
From the origins we share
Just ponder with an open mind
And consider our affection
It cannot come from contact
We seldom meet - upon reflection
When I was a teenager
I pushed you in your pram
You were too young to remember
And then our lives moved on
I loved your kind parents
Not visited often, true
But always had a warm welcome
Which I've handed on to you'

They say blood is thicker than water
But it goes deeper, far, I know
Family ties can be like junctions
Where the joining does not show
Knowledge based on the history
In the past two brothers shared

A home whose rule was kindness
A mother who showed she cared

'We are lucky that our grandmother
In Victorian times, so cold
Broke the codes that widely ruled
With a heart of purest gold'

She had great sadness, as many did
Lost five babies to illness dire
But showed the others abiding love
With gentleness that did inspire
So back beyond our time, the bond
Was forged, not one to break
Yet one that knows no urgency
As it was never ours to make
Will that connection still survive?
Our children's children never knew
Its origins or those brothers dear
Now remembered by just a few

▶ ◀

Fantasy or Reality

Fantasy or reality, stories told
Deeds and lives in past, gone days
Who knows what the future brings?
The human race must change its ways

Our world now and the one beyond
More connected, used to be
But when evil came to walk around
A veil formed, and few could see

The bridge between was destroyed
By cruel deeds and sea of pain
Those who still cause this breach
Never that far shore will gain

Sadistic pleasures, religious wars
Fanatics' ideas are spreading
Those with beliefs creating fear
On the thinnest ice are treading

One day the bridge will be rebuilt
Many centuries of time have passed
Finally, evil's power will break
Kindness will rule instead, at last

Then, only then, will the veil lift
And the bridge of light appear
For our children's sakes, let us pray
For an end to pain and fear

Fate

I awoke as I was being taken
Into a circus ring
I could hear the people shout
Scream, and even sing

I was in a horse drawn cart
For what? I did not know
But, naturally, feeling very scared
Was I to meet some foe?

Or was it to the lion's den
Chains round my hands and feet?
Was I being taken there
For the hungry beasts to eat?

Maybe a bull all furious
Released to gore and kill
Or to leave me bleeding
So mockers could have their fill

Or was a swordsman waiting
Through the gate ahead?
I could not protect myself
I was weak and under fed

I felt like a puppy
Tiny, trembling, white
Made to jump through a hoop
Of fire burning bright

Oh dear I thought,
I can't stay one moment longer
I must wake up from this dream
And then I need to ponder

I could have been helped
By those who stood to stare

But they didn't notice
And, what's more, didn't even care

I knew not the future
As I went through that gate
I only knew I was alone
To face what was my fate

Fate is unknown, mysterious
Not written by our hand
The future we try to plan
But the way not understand

So I listen to my inner self
And remember what I see
In dreams and through memories
I am learning what may be

Into the future we all go
To face what isn't shown
I only know that my behaviour
I alone must own

Fatigue

If I could sleep tomorrow
The next day or for a week
Would that ease all fatigue?
Give me the rest I seek
From pain and anguish
From all grief and tears
From anger and illness
From my memory's fears?
Would I then see the world
Through optimistic eyes?
Maybe hear nature's music?
Say no more goodbyes?

I shall dream as I sleep
Let the world within me change
And in calm green pastures
My spirit will freely range
When I awake and return
To my normal daily life
I shall have renewed vigour
To face any further strife
An empty vessel can safely meet
Neither good friend nor any foe
Gone away with this fatigue
Is the me I really know

► ◄

Fickle World

Are you only as good as your last word?
Your last action or last deed?
Everything before then disappears
So you receive not what you need
People forget effort done
Any kindness given - ignore
Give a wrong word or frown or tear
And good memories live no more

Like a football manager
When his players win the game
Becomes a national hero
And great can be his fame
Until the day no one scores
His team is now demoted
His coat must hang on another peg
And for no praise is voted

Fickle can be the world
Minds addled by drugs and beer
Unable to face the truth or worries
Disappointment or a tear
Unreal expectations born
Out of selfishness and greed
Some parents of the present day
Have spawned a shallow breed

But somewhere within the mind
A capability for pain and loss
For living through adversity
Is there, despite this mess
No amount of hiding away
Can avoid these - make no mistake
Why not just alter perspective
A happier world to make

So

Bring back endurance
Bring back caring
Bring back kindness
Bring back sharing
Bring back concern
Bring back love and truth
Bring back integrity

And accept

Life isn't always smooth

Final Destination

If the Jews want to live in Israel
Why can't they share that land
With those who lived for centuries
On the same earth tilled by hand?
Why the fighting and bloodshed?
As though both sides have first claim
They were not at earth's creation
But for their actions are to blame

What is so different?
Many others share national ground
In countries all around the world
Mixed cultures can be found
The only problem then should be
Do all together pull their weight
For peaceful co-existing?
Sadly, they often live in hate

What is the deepest problem?
Why such bitterness and greed?
Religion is often at the core
Poverty and hunger sets the seed
Deliberate pain to another
Is stored in memory deep
It cannot be erased by repentance
It belongs to the doer to keep

Life's ticket is free, but it ends
Death for all - the final fate
No altering then of life's events
When you exit through that gate
No evil is found in heaven's planes
No hurt, no fear, no greed
Those who harm another soul
At heaven's table will not feed

▶ ◀

Final Justice

The good have pain
What is the aim?
It is a shame

Something is wrong
The bad should pay
That's not the way

Those who cause pain
What do they get?
Nothing yet

But those they hurt
Have pain each day
That is the way

All memories hold
What has been
Heard and seen

At the final gate
Bad actions pay
Good wins the day

Finding Your Way

Are you on a wild goose chase and wearing yourself out?
Are you quietly asking questions?
Or do you yell and shout?
Are you looking for something? Will you know when it is found?
Are you looking in the sky?
Or searching on the ground?

What will you achieve? Will it be that for which you look?
Will it be tangible, worthwhile?
Or just ideas out of a book?
When you have it what will you do? Will it end your search?
Will you then be satisfied?
Or to a larger project lurch?

Try and seek what is your goal, then you'll have some peace
No one else can search for you.
Do you want to feel at ease?
If you say what you want, a willing helper you might find
Till you can put a name to it
It remains locked within your mind

On a rough sea, feeling sick? Make to sheltered harbour, fast
But if you are marooned and lost
Then your food will have to last
When on a journey you don't like, what difference can it make?
If you can change direction
Decide another way to take?

Travel with hope and gain knowledge, so you can recognise
What you would like to feel and hear
And clear objective visualise
Then will a search succeed. You will know where to go
Direct your life, be in control
Or drift where random winds may blow

►◄

Flowers in the Rain

A grey sky, stormy clouds
Rain batters fragile flowers
After months of slow perfecting
They are weak against its powers
Petals fall as live confetti
To the path, their beauty gone
All that effort washed away
A heavy shower, it wasn't long

They can not now return
Their time is lost forever
Another season, another crop
Old stems a knife will sever
The plant cannot feel sadness
Fortune relieves it of regrets
Because is has no memory
It neither remembers, nor forgets

But, we are different. We do both
We can withstand mere rain
We can tend the fallen plant
And help new growth to gain
But should we inflict damage
And destroy our healthy brain
Our time of beauty will be gone
Like the flowers in the rain

▶ ◀

Free Spirit in Chains

The tightness was unbearable
No air could be inspired
A moment longer and her life
Would be prematurely expired
Who was there to help her?
Who could take those chains away?
No one could find the key
Within the prison she must stay
The chains were not made of steel
But of illness long and drear
Taking freedom from the child
Breath too tight to shed a tear

A free spirit had found a home
But very few would ever know
Within those chains and hidden deep,
It rarely dared to show
But it shone an inner glow for the child
In her darkest day
Giving the path ahead a light
When there seemed no way
The flame could not be put out
Though many tried in vain
Cruelty, ignorance, prejudice
All added to the pain

The light was like a torch
Enduring for challenge great
Courage from within found
Love instead of Hate
It burned despite any storm
No power could quell its flame
She survived and gradually
For a different time could aim
The free spirit was eventually
Allowed freedom far to roam

She had learned many things
In her dreadful prison home

But the beauty of the world excelled
Despite the evil to be seen
She was glad to be alive
Though not where she had been
She never changed her nature
Her spirit made her free
Throughout the trials presented
She knew how she should be
Once well, she knew no bounds
Enthusiasm no longer caged
She worked and she played
As though time had never aged

Years had not been wasted
Despite those bonds of pain
But she vowed never to be locked
In those chains again
She understood much which others
She realised could never know
It was now her task to write the truth
Wherever the wind did blow
Now no-one would hurt her
None that road dare take
With words she fought, she was strong
Of that, make no mistake

▶ ◀

<u>Generational Change</u>

Without knowledge or medication
Before understanding's power
Damage deep and lasting
Happened within the hour
Night time pain and misery
Day time poultices to ease
But nothing and no one
Could alter most disease

Now, it is a different world
Many illnesses, we can tame
Drinking, smoking, taking drugs
Is now seen by youth as game
Destiny waiting in the wings
Pleasure takes centre stage
Writing their own nihilistic script
They will forfeit more than age

Growing Old Gracefully

I placed a rocking chair, quite big,
In a quiet, sheltered place
I found a corner of the garden
Away from the sun to face
I thought

'I shall sit, in the shade, maybe
Read the whole day through
Or possibly decide to write
A new poem or even two'

Gathering Inspiration from
The colours of the flowers
Watching the birds that call
Would pass many of my hours
In contemplation, thinking deep
Sparing time for me a while
In this way I would
Greet each day with a smile
Silence, it's true, is golden
I often like its cloak around
Allowing memories to surface
Like crocuses from the ground
In the past they were planted
Some were given little thought
Most can bloom and then die
Others just come to naught
Work and illness, hand in hand
Have taken many a day
I can now make adjustments

'But, have I the time to rock away?'

It is not within my nature
To waste time, and to be fair
I have had second thoughts
And I no longer have the chair

It wasn't very 'user friendly'
To the computer on my knee
I cannot sit just dosing
No! That isn't me
I have now the time
To do just what I choose
But I still have much to do
I must go
No time to lose

No

I shall sit a while and contemplate
And gather strength anew
Then I shall start again
~
At this age I have
Quite simply
Another and different view

▶ ◀

<u>Grown Up</u>

I understood not the silences
The frowns, the coldest glance
I could not know the reasoning
To another's tune must dance
I was too young to understand
Knew not the inner thought
My questions were all wearisome
Any answers told me naught

Then a child, now grown to be
One who walks in different shoes
A worker, mother, daughter, wife
I can do just what I choose
I answer to no one but myself
Yet, I see 'through others' eyes'
I gear my life to what they need
It is my choice
I want no prize

Hands

Hands, one source of our actions
Can be used in many ways
Gently, with care and love
Or to end a human's days
In many ways they can heal
Soothe someone who's distressed
But used with evil, they can kill
When a trigger can be pressed
A steering wheel can be turned
By an inebriated mind
If out of control with anger
Actions then become unkind

Hands that are gentle and hold
Firmly, but not tight
Have a touch that takes away
A possible need of flight
These are just the opposite
Of the ones that hurt and scar
That touch, calmness brings
Making fear disappear afar
Our hands are ours to guide
Our brains make the power flow
And the behaviour that results
Is there for all to know

'Actions speak louder than words'

Is a saying we all know
But another is more important

'We all reap what we do sow'

▶ ◀

Headache

I didn't know there were hammers
Or a vice stored in my head
Or daggers, suddenly poised to strike
But, at least I'm alive not dead

Has my brain gone briefly strange
To have such pain I wonder?
I would try to sort it out, but
My thoughts are rent asunder

I cannot think, but I'm quite sure
My brain was not for this created
It should be active and quite calm
Not feel like something grated

To be pain free seems impossible
A dream for another day
This torment is not easing
It seems to be here to stay

What have I done to have this head?
Was it something I should regret?
Oh! I cannot even remember as
The pain makes me forget

I know that when the pain has gone
Peace and quiet again reside
Then the hammers, vice and daggers
Will go back to their place to hide

I wish I knew where they were stored
I would throw them all away
So that no matter what the reason
They couldn't hurt me another day

▶ ◀

Heartache

No longer can I see your face
You are now in some other place
I do not know where you may stand
You cannot hold me by the hand
Do you call? I cannot tell
Nor hear the voice I knew so well
Gone to the orbit of eternal life
And I continue through this strife
Did you arrive early at the gate?
Or were you not allowed to wait?
Must we be separated now - for ever?
I cannot accept that fact, no, never
Our love so true will last ere long
Death cannot break a bond so strong

We shall meet, I know not when
But I shall continue on till then
Holding our memories near my heart
Our lives together in that part
An emptiness, deep, lonely, drear
Remaining so till you are near
My pain to bear, I must learn
And, maybe, one day I shall earn
The right to be with you once more
Continue on as we did before
The grim reaper took his harvest home
And left me grieving and alone
We shall meet, I know now when
Farewell, alas, farewell - till then

► ◄

Hope

Somewhere in the dark sky
I see a light.
Is it a star?
Is someone searching for me?
From wherever? From afar?

No one tells the answer
How can I possibly know?
I see a light.
Is it a star?
But, another sign must show

It is a most welcome sight
After the pall of recent years
I see a light.
Is it a star?
Shining to end all my tears?

Sent by angels from above
To flicker, so that my eye
Can see the light.
Is it a star?
No more need I try

I can think what I like
About that light.
Is it a star?
Each of us must have hope
No matter who or what we are

Hypocrisy of Religion

I went to visit Jerusalem
The city of Christ to see
Wishing to view the sepulchre
Where many bend the knee
I was eager to follow the path
Where his feet had walked
And visit places where, to crowds
The Son of God had talked

I met nothing there to mean
'Christ lived' - or even died
Only a bomb scare and much fear
It felt as though the world had lied
I saw many men dressed in black
With actions - really strange
One shut his eyes so not to see
Us visitors in his range

Others had bits of paper
On which they wrote a text
They put them into a wall
I wondered. Whatever next?
I watched, and could not believe
When they shouted without fear
Crying out fervent prayers
For dead stones to hear
No one came in white coats
To take them clear away
Now that is a miracle! I fear
It may happen to them one day

In the church the sepulchre
Was surrounded on four sides
By different churches vying
Great division there resides
What comment would Christ make?
What would he say today?

'Father, I made a big mistake
I should have left and gone away
No one understood my message
No one listened to my word
No one speaks for me here
It's as though I was not heard
My death was a waste of time
Wars rage within this land
Instead of writing all the texts
They should shake a neighbour's hand
I asked that all men should live
In friendship and in peace
Did I speak an unknown language?
As here there is no ease
Why do these men profess
To worship God and pray?
I tried to make it simple
Will they understand one day?'

I doubt I shall return to Jerusalem
Only trappings of religion I saw
Odd, irrational behaviour
Along with the grief of war
Many will disagree with me
That is their common right
But, surely, no religion should result
In pain both day and night
That cannot be God's intention
He sent his son to earth
To die by the hands of men
And time has proved his worth
Yet the message that he brought
Has been used for evil's plan
Lives still broken for selfish gain
In fact
Little has changed since our world began

▶ ◀

In Time of Need

If I need a helping hand
I will never call on you
I remember days gone by
When you refused to do
Anything to smooth my way
When I was in distress
No, I shall find another
Who will upset me less

I thought I did not deserve
Someone to guide and care
And that I would not find
The one my life to share
I believed and I decided
I would journey on my way
Doing the best that I could
On each and every day

I have found another
So faithful, true and kind
He must stand out truly
Among the world's mankind
He does without the asking
Fears not to take a stand
If I need another's help
Then I shall hold his hand

Indifference

I found I had reached a door
Leading to a different place
When I told you I saw
No reaction on your face

Through the door was beauty
It was all so light and free
But, when I showed you
You just didn't see

I walked through the door
And heard music far and near
When I asked you to listen
You didn't even hear

I wanted to share this place
Beautiful, light and free
But you never noticed
You were there with me

I returned through the door
At last I felt at peace
I had finally realised
You - I would never please

The lesson I shall remember
Your indifference matters not
My door leads to my world
To show you

Oh!

I just forgot

Inner Beauty

In the lost world of the mind
When the map of life had fled
She walked with a proud dignity
Despite the chaos in her head
Awareness of time and place
Gone as the daytime light
She had to meet each moment
From the darkness of her night

Her courage she showed quietly
Making neither fuss nor noise
Facing each day as it came
Accepting she had no choice
Unfettered by beliefs and worries
That caused her need to strife
Illness did not diminish her
In the twilight of this life

No point to question a purpose
All we knew is what had been
But the silver lining to the cloud
Her gentle, inner self was seen
Uncertain future we must meet
As we walk this earth's vast store
A beauty shone out from within
When her reason was no more

Instinct

I do not like you
I do not trust
What you do
Or what you say
Instinct tells me
Something's wrong
Your cold eyes
With me stay

What is amiss?
I can't define
The tone of voice?
Pretence untrue?
Expression's mask
Hides not from me
The dark side of
The inner you

You do not fool
You cannot change
My view of you
In others' ears
I do not speak
As I say naught
But truth 'will out'
I have no fears

A lifetime's work
To listen, watch
Little is lost
To the 'seeing' me
The smiles will go
As the darker you
Escapes from within
And others see

Interdependence

One day I know the sun will shine
I will embrace its warming ray
In the morn I'll wake to find abiding gloom has gone away

Where it has been, a mirage
Of light shall fill its space
But is more darkness lurking just ahead for me to face?

The future some may forecast
It is not in our power to know
Only the daily pilgrimage will our mortal pathway show

Are we puppets dancing to a tune?
As fate's servants pull each string
Or do we claim the future way with the results our actions bring?

Let us not blame fate or God
Though that seems easier by far
Than to accept that in this world Integrity is a star

How can we look beyond the dark?
Unless all people face the light?
Others' actions in time or place dims a glow, however bright

All we can do is journey on
Try to survive as is our right
Remember, a small candle burning gives a glimmer in the night

The future appears in the distance
Like a galaxy's twinkling view
More stars shining give a light and rekindle our hope anew

► ◄

Into Care

The grief is ever present
Yet, you are not dead
Just gone from me for ever
Hidden somewhere in your head
Unable to comprehend
Yet enough to give me blame
Knowledge of the caring years
All gone, as in one flame
Looked after now by others
Yet constant within my mind
Do they see what you need?
Are they always being kind?
Handing over practical care
Does relief replace the fear?
Giving time for enjoyment
And for others who are dear?
In reality, only sad tiredness
My heart is drained of joy
Enthusiasm, all gone away
With no energy to employ
To care or not, was not a choice
Though this legacy is great
Yet to walk along another path
Would have given a heavier weight
Life's lessons, how many more
To learn, what left to face?
When shall I feel free to roam?
And enjoy being in my own space?

▶ ◀

Is it Too Late?

You may not know till too late
When overtaken by cruel fate
That love was waiting by your door
You didn't see it on the floor
Packaged in an unknown wrap
Not dressed in frock or fancy cap

Ordinary books around us spread
No message written, no one said

'Here is the line, follow that word
On each page, a voice is heard
Telling of a love so deep'

A way to listen, you did not keep

One day, gone will be the grief
When open doors will bring relief
The closed book you dare to read
Has a memory on which to feed
The loss and anger, doubt and fears
Dissolve and smiles replace the tears

All humans can mistakes make
Lost - believing for religion's sake
Only when the truth we face
Can we live in a different place
Endless paths within our mind
Courage is needed the truth to find

► ◄

Is Life A Game?

I listen to what you say
I work through process - deep
But I wonder if you intended
Your first promises to keep?
Nothing changes, no difference seen
Endless torment just the same
Doubts and thoughts have set in
Am I just in someone's game?

A game of invisible players
Using me as the chief pawn
Moved around a massive board
Since the day that I was born
Apparently blind to my distress
Unnoticed through endless fight
The final game played on and on
Summer, winter, day and night

Who will be the Grand Master?
When this ultimate game is won
What will happen to the pawn?
When the need for her is done
It doesn't matter, it never did
As there is no choice for pawns
Just to stand where they are placed
And wait until a new day dawns

▶ ◀

Itching

An itch can start without a warning and soon it drives you mad
Once you start scratching, it becomes worse, yes, really bad
Very soon, you feel despair as you can find no ease
Cold flannel, anything, someone help me, please

Then, again, you must scratch when liniments no respite give
Creams are useless to aid. Like this – how can I live?
I cannot scratch in public or arrested I would be
No one knows the torment; it's not something you can see

I'm not discussing a mere minor irritation passing by
No, something more substantial is what I now decry
Like falling in a bed of nettles, no docking leaves to view
Or when insects in the jungle find they like your skin to chew

Going slowly, slowly crazy, hands held together tight
Can I face another day? After that last sleepless night
Nails cut short, yes, very wise, the damage - least to keep
Self control is not possible, you even scratch when you're asleep

Instead of feeling relaxed, calm, skin smooth, with mood serene
Persistent itch changes that. Devastation becomes the scene

Why were we created thus? Whatever had God to lose?
Some moments in our life we would never decide to choose

Jeopardy

Moments of pleasure, a life fell apart
Others who loved left with broken heart
What madness enters the human frame?
To jeopardise all, generations the same

The illicit love that breaks trust forever
For a marriage in ruins, good times are never
Short ecstasy fleeting, happiness given up
What makes men and women drink from this cup?

Immediate pleasure or long term content
To satisfy appetite seems the intent
But results can be felt in so many ways
And regret can last the rest of your days

In adolescence this dilemma reigns
Everyone in that phase has unbearable pains
But adult maturity should then appear
Foresight of actions helps mistakes disappear

Our lives pass by, the shadows follow
A tree is not healthy if its trunk is hollow
The leaves may have colour in the sun
But the life of the tree is nearly gone

No one can maturity or happy code teach
Human perfection we can not reach
But if common sense we can integrate
We have much less sorrow to feel and relate

▶ ◀

Joining Forces

'Would the same seem different?
If I were you and you were me
Would I change my beliefs?
See the world as you do see
Would it all feel as cold?
Or the colours be more bright?
Do you see the sunshine?
Where I just live the night'

'Life isn't fair for you
Maybe we could share it all
Both sleep through the darkness
Leave behind the fog and pall
Then when the sun rises
We both can meet each day
Walk and talk along our path
And together, forever, stay'

Journeying Together

I watched and saw them travelling
Over hill and moor, through dale
And finally along narrow water
In a small boat they did sail
Over the deep and shallows
Moving quietly along each mile
In sunshine and many winters
Together would talk and smile

But the long and winding river
Reached the ocean, a stormy day
Safe banks were lost, the mast broke
Into rough waters they sailed away
A mist enveloped the small boat
No rescue, no map, just fate
No one could help, or stop the storm
They could do naught but wait

After many harrowing days
An island did appear
They sailed, blown by the wind
To a harbour, in great fear
The elder was gently lifted off
To safety and for care
The other's place was elsewhere
She could only visit there

Many memories were collected
Along the long and winding way
Sounds to hear, to laugh, to weep
Reflections that move but stay
The fear kindly disappeared
The storm left, a haven found
Visited often to reminisce about
The journey together bound

▸ ◂

Joy

Will I ever find it?
Where can I employ?
When will I ever know
What is meant by joy?
To be free to wander
Over hill or dale?
Or, to take a deep breath
In sunshine and in gale?

When no anger surrounds me
Opposition has no sound
Hear laughter, see no frowns
Will joy then be found?
Does joy have an energy
Of its own to recognise?
Is it merely a lack of pain?
To me these questions rise

No drugs can substitute
In a life, however rough
Artificial joy is no answer
Though the path is tough
As I keep going forward
In some special place
One day I shall have
That meeting - face to face

'Joy, where have you been?
Why did you run and hide?'

'There was 'no room vacant'
So nowhere could I reside
There has to be a space
And light that you may see
Inner colours, which are my gift
With love to you - from me'

▶◀

Justice

Who can know true justice?
Of events in time and place
But people should understand
Retribution shows its face
Recorded are all actions
Nothing can be erased
Pretence has no power when
In death the veil is raised

Tremble all who are cruel
Whose action causes pain
On this earth you may hide
But mercy you will seek in vain
You will only have yourself
To blame when at the gate
You are taken straight to hell
You created your own fate

Justice may not be carried out
In the courts around the land
Sentences may not reflect
The torment from the hand
Once you reach the final door
There is no turning back
You must carry the luggage
That you alone did pack

Keeping Trust

The gradient is so very steep
To prevent a fall my efforts keep
Far away, hidden is help or aid
Weariness hides the progress made
Where do I go? Why must I stay
On this path? No other way
What can I do? No respite seen
I can't go back - that's where I've been

What lies ahead I cannot tell
But it can be no worse than hell
Pain and torment cannot last
One day they will be in the past
I shall keep going with little strength
Have I enough to go the length?
I cannot see the journey's end
Is it soon? Here? Round that bend?

Or is the path going round and round
Traversing ever the same ground?
Yet looking different, I don't know
My footsteps lost, they don't show
If I stumble then I shall fall
A chasm below - the final call
There is no other possible way
A step at a time, or here I stay

At the final gate we shall meet
What shall I say? How shall we greet?
Am I dreaming? Am I awake?
Another step forward I must make
Hope keeps a flame in sight
Small, but leading to a light
That is my belief, I know I must
Continue on - to the one I trust

►◄

Know Yourself

Whatever we do in this life, we do it on our own
We are born by ourselves, when we die we go alone
We may have people all about, with us, in the same place
But, our feelings and our thoughts, none shares that inner space
We may tell them what we think. We may share our feelings too
But they can only interpret these in our actions and what we do

No one shares another's pain but compassion helps you cope
But people get bored and tired when you sit around and mope
When you laugh, are cheerful, then others join that fun
They may even want to know the exciting things you've done
But miserable tales of painful woe - we have enough, god knows
Why should anyone want to hear or share misery that shows?

'Whatever happens, try to smile
Keep going through the gloom'

That may have been your motto, but then the dark clouds loom
If there is no one to help you walk through the vale of tears
You may stay in the sorrow and keep the pain and fears
Somewhere there is an answer. What it is and where I wonder?
Should we not feel or love and then not have the anger?

Or should we live our lives alone like the hermits did of old
Stories of living in a cave, without man or beast, are told
No, a compromise is necessary, I'll try and think one through
And when I have I'll let you know, maybe show you what to do

Till then, realise we are the same
Within, all are alone
Value that inner you
You have only yourself to own

►◄

Lasting Problems

When a sudden illness starts
Everyone is most concerned
Appropriate care is offered
Time needs not to be earned
Flowers and sympathy arrive
From unexpected friends
But soon you are forgotten
And all attention ends

Should the illness not resolve
Become chronic and remain
The sympathy disappears
'Oh! Not you in pain again'
The time and comfort melt
With no more cards and flowers
The pain and problems persist
Days and weeks pass with the hours

Eventually, the phone is silent
People no longer stay aware
The anguish remains with effort
To try to cope, still there
Our lives are given to us to live
Whatever may come our way
Struggling through may not be fun
Just 'another painful day'

Those whose lives are affected
By illness long and drear
Can get through each day
With hope and, often, fear
But we must wait, whatever
Until the reaper calls our name
Our lessons are our very own
Never two must face the same

► ◄

Latter Years

I walk the pathway of the old
Into dark and unknown deep
Daytime light becomes quite dim
While night's spectres a vigil keep
Advancing age is taking me
My care needs an extra hand
I can not stop the progress
As I watch the hour glass sand

Remember the young woman
The smile that hid the fears
The times we shared together
Through all the many years
The fading light within the mind
The door I must pass through
Leaves but the palest shadow
Of the person that you knew

Remember not sharp anger
Forget not the time and love
Given to you so willingly
When black skies were up above
A mere mortal I was born
I have lived as I thought right
Some things I see differently
As my daytime turns to night

I would stay with you forever
If time would just stand still
But relentlessly we journey on
Up life's last and awesome hill
In case I cannot understand
These words my lips not speak
'I love you, now and always'
I write them for you to keep

▶ ◀

Leaving

I miss you still. You had to leave
Your voice, your gentle smiles
The time with you made little
Of the separation of the miles
We started again where we left off
The moment we used to greet
And I shall always remember
The days when we could meet

The times we spent together
Some tears amid much laughter
These memories will appear
In my mind for ever after
Nothing can erase those images
Of good times spent with you
These are like perennial flowers
Blooming yearly, fresh and new

Life is full of moments
Some beautiful, some are bad
But all create our inner life
Though sometimes make us sad
Life is not meant to be all fun
Or else small pleasures fade
And boredom with much of life
Would our empty minds invade

I shall keep our special days
In my memory book of you
A smile or tear forever trapped
When my mood is blue to view
To transport me to better days
For a while, to a different land
I can imagine the sun is shining
In the place where you now stand

► ◄

Leaving the Nest

The children grew, years sped by
Till the time they left their home
Leaving a feeling of loneliness
Eased by contact on the phone

Some people feel they cannot wait
Till that natural time is through
We missed them, though knowing
It was something they had to do

No more of so many things
On which I will not dwell
But that time of life has passed
We carry on. They're doing well

Time together we enjoy so much
But, for a while, felt stuck in haze
Not worse, not better, just different
At the end of a privileged phase

Money, possessions - all can wait
Some people have no choice
Children can understand necessity
But
'The Joneses' have no voice

If only more people would realise
That each day is lived as new
No time can return again
And those precious years are few

► ◄

Leg Pain

Waves of pain passing down my leg
From base of spine to tip of toes
Like the sea, going on and on
Where from? God only knows

God may know but he isn't telling
So I shall just ride the storm
Pretend I fell in royal battle
When my black horse fell at dawn

Was I kicked in a childhood fracas?
Did my leg get caught somewhere?
Was I hit with a stick playing hockey?
Did it hurt like that - back there?

Maybe I jumped from a slave ship
Tried to swim the ocean wide?
A big shark espied my leg
I was washed up with the tide?

A little child wanting to run away
From what she saw as danger?
Her leg was held and she was pulled
And thrown back in the manger?

Many ideas come to mind
To help cope with this pain
I shall try to sleep and hope
It will not return again

There must be some explanation
If there is I do not know
All I feel is the awful pain
Going down from hip to toe

►◄

Legacy of Care

People look for happiness
In wealth, possessions, power
But most important is the love
That sustains from hour to hour

Never leaving for pleasure's gain
Caring through the good or bad
Travelling along the road of life
Not regretting, just feeling glad

Privileged to share in your life
Whatever that may bring
Remember that after winter cold
Come new green shoots of spring

Pain and suffering have no being
Without us they do not live
But love and care have a legacy
Warmth to the world they give

Life's Path

'What is this life?'

So many ask
This journey we all take
Is it a path already laid?
Or one that we must make
We didn't ask to be born
As far as we can tell
Life can be like heaven
Other times resembles hell
Do we travel through each day?
Follow where our instinct leads?
Or divert for another's approval?
Or to just to satisfy our needs?
Do we seek only pleasure?
Or stray from what is right?
That way we can easily turn
Our daytime into night
Or can we battle for the truth?
What is life's pain, endure?
Fight the cause and travel on
It's our choice
That's for sure

Lifetime

Life is made of waiting moments
From the beginning to its end
Not knowing what will happen
Something good or yet to mend

Something happy, something sad
We prepare as best we can
Maybe exhausting or simply bad
Like heatstroke with no fan

Some distractions can be found
In work, feelings, music, words
Or preparing food to be eaten
Or use binoculars watching birds

Drinking, smoking, wasting health
Everyone's task the same
Making decisions how to use
Time in life's waiting game

Some think they know the answers
Some tell others what to do
Adults have responsibility as
No one else can take them through

Love Messages

I had a bunch of spring flowers
Daffodils and iris blue
The message on the card read

'With love from me to you'

I had some red roses
In a bouquet through the post
The message on the card read

'I love you the most'

I had some freesias sent
On Valentines Day one year
The message on the card read

'I wish that you were here'

I had a camellia bought
In a plant pot by the door
The message on the card read

'I love you for evermore'

I have sent a message back
It's the least that I could do
It says

*'Deep within my heart I know
And I'll always love you too'*

- 81 -

<u>Maybe</u>

Maybe I cannot hear your voice
Maybe you do not speak
Maybe I do not understand
Silence is not my choice

Maybe my eyes do not see
Maybe you are not there
Maybe I miss the images
Perhaps no one waits for me

Maybe I just feel alone
Maybe you linger not
Maybe I have to accept
I am now 'on my own'

Maybe inspirations all untrue
Maybe just a lovely dream
Maybe I must manage
With mere thoughts of you

Maybe in darkness I must stay
Maybe awake the night
Maybe I can still keep hope
There is yet another day

Messages

Messages all have meaning
When another's words we hear
But actions can speak louder
Resonate both far and near
Arrangements made - excluded
Time spent but you're not there
Yet your message comes across

'Waiting for you'

But where?

Celebrations but no invitation
Alone when others meet
Yet

'I love you very much'

Over a phone, or when you greet
Choices made, with false belief
Deception can 'have a ball'
But messages become decoded
With eyes that see it all

Evidence given, excuses made
All feasible, reasonable, true
But were they the bottom line
Did those answers come from you?
No anger caused, just sadness
Such choice had to been taken
The message has its target reached
Will you find you were mistaken?

►◄

Mirage of Hope

Can you see that oasis?
With water running free
I shall be there directly
Come and you will see
Oh no! It isn't where
I thought that I would find
My eyes must be tricking me
That is most unkind

Is Hope like that mirage?
An image in the sky?
Looming in the future
'I can get there if I try'?
On arrival it isn't there
It has vanished in thin air
My mind must be tricking me
That is most unfair

The traveller journeys on
For many another day
In the heat the oasis will
Appear as though to stay
It can vanish in the ether
In the darkness of the eve
If hope really disappeared
That would be beyond belief

Monday Morning

I've never minded Mondays
It is just another day
Further work or pleasure
Whatever, it doesn't stay
Despite anything that happens
A day meets a final post
The difference is found only
In what activities we host
A day can be dull and drab
Or happy, full of cheer
Sadness can overshadow
When losing someone dear
Life isn't all enjoyment
Nor should it be all toil
But endeavour and interest
Can any boredom foil
Those who seek to avoid pain
Or run away from strife
By drugs or excess alcohol
Miss essentials in a life
No one ever likes to cry
Yet a contrast is so clear
When the sun shines after rain
Then a rainbow can appear
But if life is artificially made
To have colours every hour
They are accepted as the 'norm'
And soon will lose their power
So face your Monday mornings
With enthusiasm and new zeal
And I can assure you, truly
Much better you will feel

►◄

Moving House

Everything in a shambles
Clothes just everywhere
Cupboards emptied one by one
I wish we were already there

Boxes piled high in every room
Bits around the floor
Where does this need to go?
Sort that, and then there's more

Will we ever manage the move?
To the new house now complete
Will the van arrive in time?
Have we anything left to eat?

I must wash the kitchen floor
I cannot leave this dirt
The carpets must be vacuumed
I must change my filthy shirt

Never ending, clean and pack
What a massive, great big task

'Breakfast in bed and a rest'

I dream! But no harm to ask

'Be sensible. In this state?'

That will have to wait

▶ ◀

My Best Effort

I take vitamins
I rest in bed
I eat vegetables
I enjoy fruit
I try to be patient
Let each day go by
But, it makes no difference
All I do is cry

Time is said to be
Of healers - the best
How far must she walk?
To reach my side?
I feel like shouting

'Can you not see?
Until you arrive
My life cannot be'

Endless, continuous
There is no end
Pains come. Pains go
And I just exist
One day, I believe
Dreams can come true
I shall be well
To live life with you

I shall not stay
In this dark cloud
A daily grind
From morn to night
No I shall run
To others talk
And on different ground
I shall run and walk

►◄

My Island

A desert island just for two
No neighbours and no phone
A small productive garden
Self sufficient, on our own
No one being nasty
Isolated from the news
I could do without the world
Its people and their views
Too much prying and deceit
Fighting, hurting, illness dire
As long as I could be with you
To be free is my desire
Contact with those we love
As often as they would wish
An oven and utensils
To make their favourite dish
A computer with a battery
That lasts an endless life
Then I should be quite happy
No more anger, no more strife
To live a while our lives
Free from illness and from care
All I want and all I ask is
Free time with you to share
Walks along the beaches white
Sitting together in the shade
No tears, no coughing and no pain
To relish times that would not fade

▶ ◀

My Soul-mate

If I live to be a hundred years
That day I will remember
I saw him standing, quite alone
On the sixteenth of September
Tired, pale, resigned, no smile
Patiently he waited there

'Could I make him happy?'

Was my inner, silent prayer

Forty five years have passed
Since first I saw his face
A beautiful chord I had heard
In a deep and lonely place
In my mind it felt as though
From the past this man I knew
I'd loved and lost, then loved again
Now I know that to be true

But what shocked me even more
When I found my soul-mate, rare
I didn't know if he was free
And I thought I didn't care
He was mine, to have, to hold
To stay always by my side
Fortunately …
(Or this story would
Have been a different one to tell
As I would have walked away
Instead, deep in love I fell)
… He too had waited
This time, destiny was kind
Somehow we were guided
So each other we could find

▶ ◀

Nightmare

Always more to get through
Like a never ending stream
Of robbers or beggars taking
Continuing a similar theme

The table and chairs are broken
Disconnected mains supply
No pillow to lay my head on
No bed on which to lie

The front door, locked and bolted
No escape route could be found
Food was gone, the water off
A storm blows all around

I cannot think, I despair
Will the torment never end?
~
I wake up, thank goodness
With another day to spend

Not the Way

Down the years, like arrows
Religious beliefs their targets find
Centuries of dogma make many
Different tones in human mind
Life's meaning, like old leaves, fades
Hues and colours, none can last
But physical pain clings like ivy
When its myriads roots hold fast

Those who deliberately cause hurt
They, alone, will take the blame
Everyone's memory keeps a trace
No hiding behind 'God's holy name'
No choice is given to 'cover up'
All must meet their final gate
No 'Hail Marys', no penitent vows
Will evil actions eradicate

How do I know to write this poem?
The sensible ones should ask
Because I reached my 'final gate'
The day I nearly wore death's mask
There I learned of many things
But was not allowed to stay

'Go, write what you now know
You will be welcome - but not today'

Back to pain, but somehow changed
Evil's ways given a clearer view
'Hurt to body', its obvious tool
Religion, causing the mind to skew
Draining hope from non believers
Illegal drugs to cloud each day
The aim - that many lose their chance
Of being eternal souls one day

► ◄

Nowhere to Go

Nowhere to go
No way to turn
No escape route
No maps to burn
No forward path
Just time can move
If things can alter
Only that will prove

Can a body heal?
Can pain disappear?
Lungs learn to breath?
A mind shed a tear?
Can suffering be gone?
Is it possible in life?
Does death bring relief?
Or just further strife?

How can it be different?
Can it really change?
Pain is everywhere
With freedom to range
Over sea and continent
Travelling the air
Sent by evil anger for
Innocents to share

No respite is given
None answer the call
Equal adversity but
Different for all
No one asks to receive
What some people give
It is time to allow others
Their true right to live

▶ ◀

Old Age

I am not here just for you
Your parent I chose to be
Please fully understand
No happier one you'd see
I gave you my middle years
Willingly and with great love
That love changes not
But, before I'm called above
I have other work I must do
To fulfil my journey here
So, sometimes at present
I may not always be near
You are old enough to see
And mature to lead your life
But just remember always
I'm there in times of strife
Think not that I am selfish
Or that I leave your sphere
One day you may be proud

'She is my mother dear
She embarked along a path
On very different ground
But now I know she had to go
Something had to be found'

So my quest goes along lines
Parallel to my love for you
There are many connections
And I'm never far from view
You were always my priority
From each morn to every night
Though you make your own bed
I will still bring a needed light

▶ ◀

Our Destiny

If we decided our destiny
Would we choose our way?
To meet pain and turmoil
Each and every day
To ride the seas in the storms
Instead of by gentle breeze?
Or live our lives in poverty
Instead of wealth and ease?

My hope is that mankind
Would not consider that at all
That they would prefer sunshine
Not the dark or deepest pall
There are many black forces
They fill the world with pain
Evil rides on covered wings
Thinking our souls to gain

Those who fight for justice
Who want health and joy for all
Can vanquish evil in its tracks
Into hell the bad will fall
Then mankind will have choice
With happiness in its sight
To enjoy friendship's warmth
Or revert to endless night

Will they waste the agony?
Do the good suffer in vain?
Will drugs and greed still exist?
And cause yet further pain?
Knowledge can be used
For good or for disease
Will mankind see reason?
And find the path to peace

By air we breathe. We are connected
Interdependent, alone to cope
Dependant, yet separate for ever
A child should have peace and hope
Qualities, possessed as a right
Not something we should yearn
Earth's time, we are freely given

(But people don't seem to realise)

A place for eternity all must earn

Out Walking

Trees in their magnificence
The rivers in full spate
The valleys stretching far
The hills with ancient fate
Silence seldom broken
The curlew's lonesome call,
Sheep quietly grazing
Dark rock formations tall
The tarn beyond the hill crest
The heather in full bloom
Small paths wind ever forward
Amidst the yellow broom

To walk over any moor land
The feet are made to spring
The wind lifts the hairline
These days such joy can bring.
Walking till the body aches
The mind becomes quite free
Refreshed, relaxed and tired
That is just the way to be
A busy life of work filled hours
There I have no choice
But leisure is the open air
With Nature's own clear voice

► ◄

Outcomes

Life's journey is a gift to all
But the future is never shown
Where you go, what you want
Your behaviour you must own
You have memories to look at
On experience you can feed
Your ageing path is quite unique
Try to find the help you need
You can listen or can ignore
But by your actions you can lose
Or you can gain true happiness
What you do is yours to choose
Do not blame others if an outcome
Is not what you had in mind
They are not your keepers
The right pathway you must find
To discuss and then discuss more
Only attempts to understand
Look instead for what you want
Take steps to that different land
You are no longer a young child
At the mercy of those you meet
No, you are grown up and now
Go forward each day to greet
Old habits learned in difficult times
In childhood play no part
Your outcome in all areas
Is yours. So why not make a start?
Happiness waits behind the wings
Dressed in many a different guise
Take off myopic glasses
And be prepared to recognise

► ◄

Parents

We all go through childhood
We are not given preparation
We arrive in a certain place
Our parents we have not chosen
We do not decide for ourselves
Whether we are rich or poor
It is as though we are simply
Pushed through an open door

For all children, home should be
A nurturing, learning place
One where abilities flourish
And confidence grows apace
Before that door is opened
Before they see their child arrive
Parents should just sit and think
How to help their child to thrive

Parenthood is for a lifetime
Not just the first few years
A commitment of being there
To prevent hurt and comfort tears
The neuroses of adult life
Usually date back to the child
To traumas that have happened
When their young world went wild

A child needs to be safe and know
That parental love endures
Only time will build the trust
Which effort and love secures
If you cannot give the time
The effort and the love
Then you should not cause a child
To leave its heavenly home above

All will have to answer
For their actions through the years
No one can avoid all pain
Or prevent all their children's tears
We have our own path to tread
But a parent has an extra role
The biggest responsibility on this earth
That of caring for another soul

A task too onerous to just cast off
Or ask someone else to do
If you brought a child into the world
Then you should guide it through
Its early years - of learning
Its teenage years - to separate
Help it to cherish others
To love and never hate

▶ ◀

Patience

Patience, virtue, is a flower
Gentle as a breeze that blows
Cooling the fever of the brow
When the waiting time it knows
The heat from a searing sun
Merely makes its colour bright
Cheering up a tedious day
With its ray of coloured light

Patience, necessity, is different
No gentle flower is she
Neither sloth, asleep all day
A tenacious wild cat she must be
Sharp claws clinging to the tree
Of life, lest she should fall
Hissing at any who dare to pass
Ignoring those who call

Patience has no finite length
Overstretched - her colour pales
Mirages of hope conjured to view
Disappear as progress fails
Yet, though no longer caring
She keeps going, despite all
She will never let another down
Nor in despair's clutches fall

A chameleon, changes with the light
So, with events of life, must we
Patience waits for time to pass
In whichever mode she has to be
The tree that sways in the wind
Keeping roots secure and fast
Will better 'ride through the storm'
Till calm peace returns at last

► ◄

Poem for a Young Mum

'Mummy, why are you crying?'

*'Because I am very happy
I never thought that I would have
A chance to change your nappy'*

'Mummy, why do you frown?'

*'Because I feel quite sad
That a lot of other mothers
Cannot care and be as glad'*

'Mummy, why do you smile?'

*'Because I love you so
And I shall be with you for years
As you thrive and as you grow'*

'Mummy, why do you laugh?'

*'Because I find you funny
Your little ways are endearing
Your skin smells sweet as honey'*

'Mummy I do love you
I am happy when you are near
I want to make you laugh not cry
Please! Do not shed a tear
As I am here for you now
Your waiting days are gone
But I know that your love for me
Will grow and be so strong
That you will guide me safely
And the kindest Mummy be
I will be the happiest child
That you could ever see'

Poem for Smokers

Just a word or two
~
To those who smoke
This message is for you
It will soon be too late to stop
The damage that you do
To your two healthy lungs
Each day you give abuse
But one day you may regret
The results of your misuse

Not only can you not breathe
But damaged lungs give pain
And a feeling like drowning
Much restriction you will gain
No longer walking freely
Coughing as the days go by
To run or dance impossible
No breath to even cry

How do I tell you this?
I know it from all my life
Born with lungs that react
With restriction, giving strife
But if you give no thought
Wasting your precious health
Then I can assure you now
There is no point in wealth

Nothing can compensate
New lungs you cannot grow
When you find you have the pain
Then too late the message know
Cancer is not the only end
Subtle changes will appear
Closing the small bags for air
One by one they disappear

No more time spent having fun
Your loved ones suffer too
When you are dying early
Grieving is all that they can do
For some momentary pleasure
People give their lives away

'That is my choice'

I loudly hear

'My life is mine''

You say
Ignorance you cannot plead

'I did not know or realise'

*'That excuse we do not heed
The dangers were spelled out
Clearly, for many years
Our gift of life had little value
You move us not by tears'*

What could happen then?
That answer I do not know
But if you throw back a gift
Usually another one won't show
Life here can be hard and dire
Or filled with love and joy
Whatever else comes with the gift
Choice is there for our employ

▶ ◀

Power of Love

Out of sight of every angel
Hidden from all heavenly view
In a dark and lonely place
I keep going, just for you

Endless pain my companion
Despair tries to hold my hand
'Go away', I do not falter
As one day with you I'll stand

Love is much more powerful
Than fear, however great
And pain will never conquer
Though to suffer is my fate

Heavenly love abides forever
Beyond the darkness, deep
And angels wait, anxiously
A constant vigil keep

They cannot help nor remove
The anguish within my mind
But my soul is supported
So, my spirit, strength does find

Evil will never rule this earth
Though they try by pain and fear
Why? Because love is stronger
And I love you, my dear

▶ ◀

Preparing for the Final Farewell

I feel grief at your leaving
Though, as yet, you are around
Treading the same pathways
On this solid, earthly ground
Mortals fight and kill and maim
Where wild flowers grow
Showing hate instead of love
Evil's influence to show

No limit to your devotion
Or the help and care you gave
Walking through arid desert
You were sent, at last, to save
No one knew of your existence
Or would truth credence give
That an angel sent from heaven
Could through another live

Now the time approaches when
You will not come to our door
The penalty of your success
We shall see your face no more
You will go back to your home
We mere mortals live our fate
After life we will meet again
With patience, we shall wait

Quiet Vigil

Quietly I sit, what does she know?
Awareness, rarely now can show
A vigil I keep, many hours each day
However long?
Till she finds her way

What does she think? Where is she?
Her mind is not with me
What places visits, journeys makes?
Who does she hear?
Whatever see?

As I watch, I notice, now and then
A smile lights up her face
Yet she cannot tell me
Who is there
Or in what place

But, despite her condition
She seems, somehow, at peace
Waiting for the final door
And then
Everlasting ease

I shall not know, she cannot say
Those mysteries none can speak
When we reach the final gate
Too late
Our destiny to seek

Life is given to all on earth
Our mind and will dictate
Heaven waits for those who love
Hell's door opens
For all who hate

▶ ◀

Realisation

I believed you loved me
And I was wrong
My soul now weeps
But it is strong
All was pretence
It was not true
Yet despite all
I still love you

Though years pass
And your face fades
Sadness wakens
From the shades
Did I know
My belief was wrong?
Is that what made
Me so strong?

Realisation brought
Pain and tears
But no longer dread
Or any fears
I coped without
Your guiding love
And I now believe in
A heaven above

A force much higher
Of greater worth
Than missing love
From here, on earth
You will remember
That your life through
You were blind to
My love for you

►◄

Reality not Dreams

Were you made of hardened wood?
From, perhaps, a dead oak tree?
Your mind unable to respond
To the suffering you could see

Were you made of toughened metal?
Shining bright, in stainless steel?
Your body resilient and strong
But in your heart you did not feel

Were you made of solid glass?
Transparent to the watching eye?
Yet from within you could not hear
When a child was made to cry

You did not realise I was from
A different mould from you?
A soft more flexible material used
Unknown, from your rigid view

I would travel to far off lands
Find in Kashmir a mountain goat
And fashion you from its wool
As if a comforting winter coat

You would protect and keep me warm
When winds blow and frost is cold
And I would love and care for you
When threadbare and getting old

Dreams are but useless wishes
To indulge only brings regret
You did not fashion yourself, alas
So, I accept your path was set

▶ ◀

Reflections

People seek to know the truth
Can chose either wrong or right
But who makes our decisions
To live in peace or die in fight
When minutes have ticked away
As will happen to one and all
Those who decide for others
Will have to answer at the call

If no one made cigarettes
If no one made the guns
If no one made the chemicals
If no one made the bombs
If no one hurt another
If children could walk free
If the surplus food was given
If all wars ceased to be

Beyond the chasm separating
This life with all its fears
There is room for everyone
Who has not caused evil's tears
A world with never ending time
Where the wicked don't exist
Yet the puzzle here is unresolved
As to hurt others some insist

Are they stupid or simply mad?
They will reap what they give out
Those who feel the pain know well
What it's like to scream or shout
The terrorist leaders of this world
Hide as cowards to the end
Innocents go to their deaths
But themselves they do not send

Why not? If the doctrines
They belief are really true
First on the ship, lead from the front
Is what they'd want to do
But hiding, running, in disguise
They should know they live in error
They are simply waiting to
Spend their eternity in terror

Forgiveness for minor offences
All humans make mistakes
That is the fragility of our lives
Its cost the owner takes
But for actions quite deliberate
Mercy will not exist
When face to face with judgement

'Too late'

Those powers insist

'You knew what you were doing
Yet you kept on just the same
You enjoyed giving others pain
Now you give yourself the same
We do not hand out mercy
No! You reap what you have sown
All must learn the lesson
Pain you give, so you must own'

I see a world in a future time
No bombs, no drugs, no wars
Everyone working for each other
Not creating further scars
Everyone living in freedom
Exploitation in the past
Fearless during day or night
True peace on earth at last

Not peace dependent on meetings
Under duress or counted votes
Or money passed around as bribes
Or from scribbled, uneasy notes
But out of a deep true kindness
For all children women bear
Birth control in every land
Children safe, in love and care

It can be done, gradually
When people work and care
To bring a rightful legacy
To all whose world we share

Regrets

No regrets about my age
No regrets about belief
No regrets about who I am
That is a big relief
But I do have regrets
About the body in which I live
It has had too much pain
With nothing left to give

I wish that I had been given
The energy and time to be
A better friend and companion
To those who care for me
Restrictions have enveloped
This life since I was small
Had I been free, those whom I love
Could have had it all

I have regrets, yes many
About things I could not do
People I could not be with
Days and weeks to struggle through
But regrets are wasted moments
Things that cannot be undone
Times you never can have back
Opportunities long since gone

If I had created my destiny
Health would 'first priority' be
But I have just had to accept
Someone thought this right for me
I cannot argue, I do not know
Who gave me this life to live
But, when we meet, I shall tell him
I had so much more to give

▶ ◀

Rejection

When you've given of your all
When you are tired, fit to fall
What pushes you beyond recall?
Rejection

When your love is often blind
And you seek peace of mind
What do you not want to find?
Rejection

When at work you battle through
Trying hard your tasks to do
Ambition denies loyalty to you
Rejection

Unhappiness comes from all deceit
Jealousy's green eyes you greet
Truth and trust they cannot meet
Rejection

Your values you must keep in sight
When you see emotion's night
Then one day you will have light
Without rejection

Rejection is based on action's weak
That selfish man may wish to reek

'Who shall inherit but the meek?'

Accept rejection

Those who do not goodness know
Within a beauty will not flow
What then do these people show?
Rejection

Resignation

Is this how I am to be?
Restricted, tired, weak?
Not the one you cherish?
Not the one you seek?
I don't know any longer
Time passes on its way
And I am left, wondering
What to do another day

I have tried very hard
Daily, my life through
Nothing have I avoided
Though much was hard to do
Yet, all has meant nothing
When balanced in the scales
Forgotten effort wasted
And my endeavour fails

So, I am left, I feel lost
Had the journey any point?
Or was I just deluded
That my head you would anoint
I doubt I shall ever hear
Your voice. You will not call
To simply say 'well done'
Or even 'you did not fall'

No matter, I have no regrets
I have done my very best
And I can hold my head up high
Along with all the rest
I have decided - I shall walk tall
My boat will never sink
I shall continue to travel on
Despite what you may think

► ◄

Resolved

If only I had known
Your love a vigil kept
Then would my anguish
Have eased as I wept
But I only felt the pain
Day after endless day
No comfort, no relief
Grief had come to stay

Why did I ever doubt
Except I had no choice
I couldn't see you at all
Nor could I hear your voice
But now I know the truth
The reason understand
I can sleep again in peace
Knowing you hold my hand

In dire times you were there
Invisible to my eyes
A fragrant smell noticed
A warmth was your disguise
But now I can follow
Where your feet may lead
Knowing I shall safely walk
And in green pastures feed

Responsibility

What reply will you give?
When time comes to atone
For your actions on the earth
You must answer all alone

'I was too busy'

Or maybe

'I didn't really care'

At that time all knowledge
You will have to share
No hidden secret thought
No evasion, no excuse
Only the truth allowed
To the listening muse
Then it will be too late
To repair any damage done
Like a wave, time moves on
Opportunities missed have gone
In heaven is understanding
Of deep fears that will unfold
When past doors are opened
Though the locks are very old
No more challenge will you meet
As at the master's knee you sit
When you reach the final door
Will you have the key to fit?

►◄

<u>Responsible Love</u>

No one ever made me
Work so hard and long
No one tried to force me
To go on and on and on
What would have happened?
If another way I'd taken
I shall never know
Maybe I was mistaken
Should I have put my feet up?
Rested in pastures green
I could have left no trace
That I had ever been

There are some things in life
Which mean more than pain
So I made myself carry on
For those I had to gain
No other needs to know
No other needs to share
In whatever I endured
I did! That's all I care
No one ever made me
Fight so hard and long
But for you I made myself
Go on and on and on

Retirement

In my many working years I had gadgets by the score
Some to clean, some to cook all intended to do a chore
A vacuum cleaner's music as it collected all the dust
In my household the latest dust-filter was a 'must'
My first automatic washer was so wonderful to see
Like a theatre show I watched. Hours of freedom given to me
A food processor was needed for the veggie chopping
And a two wheeled trolley for doing weekly shopping
Electric whisk for puddings, machine for making bread
Books of recipes and pictures, though seldom were they read

Embroidery is out again
The Internet I now can surf
My car is washed by hand
Garden projects I unearth
No more alarm clock ringing
No more wiping off the frost
No more fearing snow or ice
No more getting lost
No more telephone ringing
No more letters to be done
I enjoyed all my work
But I'm not sorry it has gone

No more racing through the day now my working life is past
Despite old age, retirement is good, so long may it all last!

▶ ◀

Return to Jerusalem

Christ returned to Jerusalem
Two thousand years had fled
Since he was crucified and died
So he found a room and bed
He was woken from a deep sleep
The bomb gave him a fright

'What on earth is happening
In the middle of this night?'

Christ walked, no one knew him
To a village six miles away

'Would you like a refreshing drink?'

He heard a young girl say

'We are not rich. We have no wealth
But the sun is so hot today
You are welcome to rest awhile
No bombs have come this way
We still have my father's house
Home of many generations
So have a seat, while you can
Soon there may be altercations'

'Thank you, I accept the offer
Of a little wine and bread
Fish is fine, you are so kind
Please, explain what you have said'

'The Palestinians want to live
In their land, it was never sold
Others gave some for the Jews
I was not born. I have been told
They all fight. Many are killed
Our lives are full of fear'

'You still retain your kindness
That, to me, is very clear'
Why do so many Jews wish to live
In Jerusalem and around?'

'Don't you know Christ died here?
They believe it's hallowed ground'

'Oh, but he didn't die for this
For fighting, hate and greed
He wanted nations to show love
And all the hungry feed'

(Then to himself he said)

'I spent those dreadful, cruel days
Fastened to a cross of pain
I might as well have enjoyed my life
As nothing has come as gain
I have travelled around the world
Everywhere it is the same
Atrocities, fighting, hate and wars
Actually done in my 'holy 'name

Where did I make the big mistake?
People believe in me, that's true
But my life made things even worse
That's not what I meant to do
It's become the wrong way round
They think belief in me will save
But my example of love and care
Is the message that I gave'

▶ ◀

Role of Religion

Religions hold the world in thrall
While we, mere mortals, plod
Priests may read the scriptures
But know not 'the mind of God'
Then, because they are ordained
Given fancy robes to wear
People believe it is 'the truth'
In all sects - everywhere

From books of rules and stories
Written many centuries past
Come wars, pain and bloodshed
With dire effects that last
Only ideas conceived by men
Could let women lose the right
To freely walk and show a face
Instead, many live in endless night

But, religion's chosen few will die
The beliefs then have no powers
They, just like all men everywhere
Must account for earthly hours
Forgiveness is not theirs to give
Absolution not in their 'brief'
Behaviour is recorded in the mind
How can they bring relief?

Don't be fooled by 'easy' words
Or brainwashed due to fears
All must answer for themselves
When the final gate appears
Religion is not the path to heaven
The answer is for us to find
Have goodness in your heart
Care for others and be kind

►◄

Sadness of Loss

I question why I am so sad
As I knew your time was near
I sat with you while you left
And did not shed a tear
I was only concerned that you
Were without pain or fear
I held your hand, just in case
You knew that I was near

Now that reality has come
It is like a different place
I cannot talk again with you
Nor ever see your face
I only remember you as old
Frail, weary, too tired to live
After a year of illness
You had nothing left to give

I wish I could recall when
With energy and more to spare
You were a young mother
Though anxious about our care
But at this time the curtain
Has fallen on those past years
Maybe the memories will return
When time stops all the tears

▶ ◀

Silence

Silence can be golden
And such a wondrous joy
When away from noises
Which continue and annoy

Silence can be silver
In a moonbeam's light
When standing close together
In the middle of the night

Silence can be icy cold
When no other speaks
When contact is cut off
And it goes on for weeks

Silence can be present
In a mind that is at peace
One that resolves conflicts
Or views the world with ease

Silence can be for ever
When someone goes away
Their last earthly journey
One moment in one day

Sleepless Night

'New morning' is here
Not a moment too soon
The night has passed
Just watching the moon
I've done this before
The steps I must mount
Reach high as a mountain
With one endless fount
As, it wasn't the snoring
Or anyone crying
I didn't hear owls
Or cats caterwauling
No traffic noise entered
My room in the night
I wasn't disturbed by
A neighbouring light
No, I was awake
Trying to cope with disease
Screaming within didn't
Make the pain ease
Only total exhaustion
Brought respite at last
Not for long, though
Night perils are past
It will all end one day
And a different world be
When 'new morning' for others
Includes even me

▶ ◀

Some Thoughts on Religion

Now, understand
I'm not a philosopher or cleric
I don't pontificate or shout
But it behoves us all to think
Use our minds to sort things out
The main religions in the world
Make dogmas for 'all men'
They interpret old written words
But, who wrote the words back then?

Men, whose ideas had influence
Were allowed to write and read
They wrote the scriptures from their view
While others did their bias heed
In many religions women are given
A low, subservient place
Do men really think that God
Would accept this with good grace?

From beliefs in the written word
Much harm has caused to be
Passed down for generations
A rethink we need to see
Clerics may have good intentions
Hell's road was paved that way
But look elsewhere for the truth
Spiritual planes are there to stay

In this world over centuries by
Men of religious conviction
More damage and pain have been caused
Than from all disease or infection
For fighting wars and causing terror
An excuse of 'god's name' is given
But, cruelty, oppression and prejudice
Will lead to hell, not heaven

Someone

Someone could tell you. Someone who knows
I lived a busy life which a tired face shows

Someone can tell you. Someone who cares
I travelled a path of pain and I paid the fares

Someone can tell you. Someone who can see
On the way I have found a quite different me

Someone can tell you. All may say the same
But now, I don't try to remember your name

Those who have crawled across bleak, cold terrain
Can describe the images that in my brain remain

Someone can tell you. But it will not be me
As you are now amongst the ones I don't see

Someone can tell you. It wasn't my choice
But I have forgotten the sound of your voice

Those who did not care or to my pain were blind
Have disappeared in crevices deep in my mind

Someone can tell you. One who loves me more
I have no energy left or the will to explore

Enjoy your life day to day. I shall not play a part
Something was broken by the pain. It was my heart

▶ ◀

Temper

Anger presents in many ways
Which do you recognise?
If you are able to explain
Then you are getting wise

Do you want to scream and shout?
Do you want to have a fight?
Do you let the anger out?
But you know that isn't right

Maybe it suddenly appears
Like a tornado, storming through
Whatever, you can change your ways
That's something all can do

What makes your temper appear?
Was it something someone said?
Did you feel upset 'inside', but
Show anger - 'outside' – instead?

Next time you feel angry
Or have a 'tantrum' flare
Try to think what caused it
There are other ways to share
Your thoughts and your feelings
Without a big 'to do'
You are left feeling 'in the wrong'
When you lose control of you

We learn to speak quite early
Use words to sort things out
Use intelligence to understand
Then you'll have no need to shout

The angry feeling could be
In the middle of your head

In your stomach or your chest
And by injustice may be fed

Others who do not feel your pain
May not understand your ire

But, truthfully

'Temper' after the age of two
Can make even Patience tire

Thoughts on the 23rd Psalm

Is the Lord my shepherd?
Did he then forget his crook?
Where were the green pastures?
I did not see a gentle brook
A total absence of still waters
Nowhere could I lay my head
Only the Valley of the Shadow
Of Death appeared instead

Different pains made my path
No angels helped the fears
An arid journey, hard and long
Only watered by my tears
I felt no comfort nor had a rod
As I journeyed on my way
The staff of life nearly broke
Goodness had strayed away

As I travelled ever onwards
Mercy was kept well hidden
At the house of many rooms
To partake I was not bidden
To you, oh Lord, with your flock
I'm invisible. You could not see
No protection was around
Deaf to any prayers from me

I survived, I am quite tough
I bear many scars of strife
Enough to realise the truth
Religion is just a crutch in life
Words that can bring a tear
When set to music's charm
But only caring behaviour
Will keep any child from harm

▶ ◀

The Answer

I have been told the answer
To a mystery that will evolve
Many people will suffer pains
No one and nothing can resolve
The highest and the lowest
Those powerful on this earth
Who, with hate, inflicted pain
Will all finally learn their worth

How have I the courage to say this?
I was taken to heaven's gate

'Return to suffering'

I was told

*'So evil ones will know their fate
The journey of truth is over
Hell's doors are now open wide
Those who have hurt others are
Having a preview of what's inside*

*The pain they have inflicted
Actions stored within their mind
All from memory are released
And themselves the target find
Drug pushers suffer 'withdrawal'
Paedophiles - childs' anguish feel
Those who have released terror
Their own pain will make them kneel
Wars, destruction, and cruelty
Will cease - no progress made'*

Then, on floors I saw people
Rolling in pain that will not fade
Fanatics have themselves to blame
As their minds and hands created

All the pain they now feel
Because in this world they hated
The message of love was given
Two thousand years ago
People did not listen. Evil's plan
To dominate was carried through

But a band of higher spirits
Was sent from God on high
To defeat all evil on this earth
Quite a task for them to try
Love, Peace and Justice
Equality, Truth and Grace
Came with Mercy, the daughter
Whom God sent to this place
Evil killed them many times
No leniency, no reprieve
The worst pains and cruelty
Many times they did receive
Enduring torture and horrid deaths
Many lives were passed this way
Gathering suffering to themselves
So evil's pain would stay

But in the final painful lifetimes
All those agonies were felt again
The pain could now be taken back
To Hell, the store for evil's pain
The task has been completed
And the world can start to change
As love, not evil, will be abroad
Over all the world to range

'Hurt not or you will receive
The pain back, but with no end'

This message I was asked to give
So this poem to all I send

▶ ◀

The Cage of Asthma

The bars are immoveable
The cage is far too small
No movement is possible
A fractional inch - that's all
No animal would be enclosed
Yet no one can take me out
No one can find the door
And I cannot even shout

What shall I do? I shall go mad
I can't bear to stay in here
Let me out! Let me out!
Is there no one there to hear?
The voice shouts only in my head
There is no breath to waste
How long will I survive?
Someone! Please come in haste

But no one is around
No one has any notion
There is no key, no access
And I haven't any option
I cannot break the bars
They are as hard as steel
The pain is taking over
That is all that I can feel

'Time is passing',

My mind says

'Just count as the minutes go
If you bravely carry on
You surely will get through
Try to relax, think other thoughts
Picture places, happy days'

That is fine for a short while
Again panic comes and stays

'There are a lot of strategies
Try not to care, try not to fight'

'That's all very well,'

I reply

*'But I cannot breath. It is too tight
Just let me out! Just let me out!'*

Within there is despair
I need to breathe!
I have to breathe!
All I want is some new air

*'I don't want your strategies
I don't want to relax or fight
I don't want to be in here
Let me out! Just get it right!
Break the bars, do something
For goodness sake! Just break this spell
Give me some space to move
And deep breaths of air as well'*

If only I could escape
I would run far away
As far as possible from the cage
But it's attached. There is no way
It has been manufactured
Just for me and I cannot sell
The rib-cage was aptly named
It is my very own 'cage in hell'

▶ ◀

The Driver

The bus travelled along the road
Like a relic from the past
Shabby, scratched and very worn
Much longer it will not last
The driver in the cabin
Travels from place to place
No one takes any notice
No one sees his tired face

Over rocky mountain track
A tyre needs repair
The driver alone, with no help
Has to fit his only spare
Meanwhile for the passengers
Refreshments, coffee, tea
No one takes any notice
No one hears the driver's plea

The passengers have a swim as
By a lake the road now winds
Water soothes and cools them
Renewed energy each finds
The peace and beauty of the place
Adds an element of charm
No one takes any notice
When the driver feels alarm

The storm clouds gather up above
The wind begins to blow

'It it time to leave this place
Be quick, for we must go'

The passenger's look up to see
Who commands attention so
They have to take notice now
The driver they must know

- 134 -

The face seems quite familiar
The voice they have heard before
How strange, the puzzle lasts
Until they find out more

'I have driven you many times
You have travelled the road with me
But you have never noticed
I was the same. You didn't see
Through the Valleys of the Shadows
Over the Mountains of Fear we sped
On narrow ledge and icy road
I managed to keep my head
But no one noticed the driver
Invisible, I battled on
I drove you there, every time
Now my working days are done
Another driver you must find
To follow more roads, so steep
No other driver would even try
To traverse dense forests deep
If you decide you want to travel
Then, before you leave your base
Please, just notice the driver
It will no longer be my face'

▶ ◀

The Final Harvest

Time passes, personal moments
Generations have had their day
For everyone the same process
Different experiences on the way
Many suffer times of anguish
Some have fortune or good health
But most plod through daily strife
Old age approaches all with stealth
The arms of wealth enclose some
Gathered together by fate's own hands
But happiness cannot be bought
Nor be found where evil stands
When we answer, as all must do
The questions at the final door, shall we be told

'You did well' or

'You should have done much more
Your chance on earth is over
The past you can not change
You must now learn, just go that way
Over your lifetime you will range
If you can learn and see the truth
You will come back this way
But should you not
Then these doors forever locked will stay
You are not bad. You just did not use
The abilities you were given
You had many when some had few
But by other needs were driven'

Time passes, personal moments
Generations have faced their maker
All actions known, each goes the way
Of the giver or the taker

▶ ◀

The Good Shepherd

We are told of the Good Shepherd
Tending his flock by day and night
Vigilant at all times
His legacy one of light
Safe keeping, reliable
Watching over all his sheep
But, we hear, one lamb strayed
Did he lapse and go to sleep?

If he was watching carefully
And kept his lambs close by
Why did he not notice
The one that passed him by?
Taken by a wolf, dressed up
In sheep's clothing, very clever
Why did he not see the signs
Of that dastardly endeavour?

Does a wolf have similar stride?
Hold its head in a same way?
Did he not hear the little lamb
Bleat with distress that day?
He may have searched a long time
As a caring shepherd would
But should it have happened?
Can you call the shepherd 'good'?

It's human nature to make error
Everyone can make mistake
No one can be perfect
Super powers that would take
So accept that the shepherd
Tried hard and did as well
As any other, but don't belief
All the stories people tell

▶ ◀

The Invisible Picture

The picture had been painted
In long-since days of yore
Faded from the sight of men
As though not there before
Yet beneath the veneer
Of a paper, blank to view
Was a history of many lives
That none on earth now knew

Slowly walking along her path
Her days turned into night
In dire illness, she felt much pain
But the darkness honed her sight
She had stumbled into the picture
As she fell, was hurt and cried
It was too much, the tears flowed
Though brave, she could have died

'What shall I do?'

She asked herself

'How can I more pain survive?
No one knows this different place
Will not know I'm still alive'

She cried, as never she wept before
Her tears flowed like a river
In the picture all were bathed
She saw, and in fear did shiver

Witnessing cruelty beyond belief
To innocents, unprotected
Grief that never could resolve
To these victims she connected
Her tears washed every corner

Their pain, once felt, was gone
She released them from history
She now knew her path was won

As she shed the tears, she saw
Many lives in different places
But the characters were the same
They had similar inner faces
The good were good. Bad were bad
Only years of time were changed
They would not be erased again
In her memory they were arranged

She gradually left the picture
As the way became quite clear
She took the good and the brave
To those who loved them dear
Waiting in the heavens above
Angels' choirs sang with joy
The bad could then be judged
By the pain of their employ

The gates of hell were opened
From far distance she had a view
Protected by a shield of love
But, now, at last she knew
Hurt caused, like a magnet
Pulled the bad beyond the flame
To feel forever the pain they caused
In the hell from whence they came

The Leaving

She left with little warning
Together, then life was gone
Eyelids stilled all movement
No breathing. Death had won

Yet victory to her belonged
Without fear in her final hour
A brief encounter with a pain
But it had no power

I would ask that when I die
I could have a similar fate
Holding hands with one I loved
Never early but not late

She was there one minute
The next - I started sorrow
No more to talk or walk with her
We shall not meet tomorrow

She died before her body
Became too burdensome to carry
Heaven knew that she was weary
And no longer made her tarry

I said goodbye. I kissed her
Stroked her forehead. Combed her hair
With face serene, she had gone
She had nothing more to share

▶ ◀

The Lost Opportunity

Through desert, bog and cruel storm
I have searched for many a year
Trying to find the one I lost
Hoping again a time to share
I did not know where to start
No voice heard, no face was seen
Wherever life has taken me
The quest has forever been

I trusted that you felt the same
So close, before, were we
I thought that any time you could
You would try to contact me
That both striving to the same goal
Some progress we would make
And one day, if we kept going
Find a message we could take

Now I have been sad and I cried
I've been told you made a call
You know my name and number
But to my ears none did befall
I understand that when you went
No choice was yours to make
My quest would seem invalid
If opportunity you don't take

I wonder if it was your choice
Of if there was no option
You may need a brief respite
I really understand that notion
But the contact I have suffered for
And longed for since my birth
Would pointless be, if willingly
You waste any time on earth.

After the anguish was finally shed
I realised you were given a duty
To bring me to the green fields
To a place of calm and beauty
Someone who conversed with you
Told me of your equal tears
If so your action was for the best
I must forget rejection fears

The Memory of a Mother

I stood before her coffin
Gave her flowers for one last time
Remembered she had been so old
And how pretty in her prime
She walked this earth with dignity
Her counsel was kept, her own
Many thought they knew her
Within she was secret and alone
Skilled in listening with interest
What person did others know?
The face showing on the surface
Was not always the one below
Lacking confidence, with anxiety
She aimed to be right and fair
Religious belief kept her blind
To question she did not dare
When in the last year of her life
Her mind was stripped and bare
Earth's toiling gone, a beauty
Was released, and she was there
She would have a look of serenity
A confident smile of love
She saw what others seldom see
Those in a plane above
I kept a vigil for many years
Striving to do the best
I could cope with a surface scratch
Love needed no behest
I stood and faced her coffin
Said goodbye and felt sad pain
A thought came into my mind
'Grieve not. You will meet again'
Warm comfort touched my heart
Someone stood with me
A cool arm my shoulders felt
'Her spirit lives. She is now free'

▶ ◀

The Mission

Is it possible? Is it reasonable?
Can the human mind ever find
A way to conquer evil?
To the benefit of mankind

Evil comes from a plane
None in this world can trace
Hidden in the deepest black
No one can its deeds erase

Quietly, surviving for eternity
In spiritual realms above
Love from beyond the grave
Descends gently, as a dove

No one sees its image
No sound it makes in flight
This love can conquer evil
And people will see its light

When into hell the wicked go
Pulled by their cords of pain
They will never more return
To sully the earth again

The Nightmare

The boat broke its anchor
In the silent dark of night
Only one lay sleeping
She awoke before the light
A storm was wildly raging
And the wind howled loud

'When I went to sleep
There wasn't even cloud'

The rain fell in torrents
Fearing to fill the boat
She, alone, with no help
Felt constriction in her throat
No use to shout, no one there
None to offer aid
She must just battle on
Her courage must not fade
How? Why? Who had caused
Such calamity, such fears?
Danger so terrible
She wept her anger's tears

She grasped the side of the boat
With a strength as yet unknown
And prayed until the wind
Had its last journey flown
Daylight came with no sight
Of land, north, west or east
South, just the horizon
No hope, but calm at least
The sun shone with no pity
Skin burned, and mouth so dry
She could do nothing
But wait, wait more, then cry
Then she heard someone
Speak, as if inside her head

'I am with you. Just hold on
You'll not yet be with the dead'

A ship, sailing by, espied
Her jumper of bright red
And, to cut a story short
She was saved, and in her bed

Had she had a nightmare?
While sleeping in the night?
I only know, that storm was real
And she had won her fight

▶ ◀

The Oasis

A quiet place to stay and think when a busy day is through
Gives the mind a welcome break when there is nothing left to do
Sometimes along our pathways the days are rushed and loud
No respite from decisions and no breathing space allowed

I found a woodland pathway, rhododendrons by the walk
Only the sound of songbirds, but no chatter and no talk
Then strolled along a river bank, listening as the water flowed
I really do believe no more soothing record could be sold

I keep that oasis of quiet thought stored in memory in my mind
A place that I can visit, when time to travel can not be found
I go there in my imagination. I just shut my eyes and see
A view that I love really best and become as calm as I can be

My way costs no money, takes little time, is good for health
It works for young and old alike and those with little wealth
Some people need to hear loud noise to know they are alive
Like water in an oasis, I need peaceful quiet to survive

The Ornate Gate

I was told in days gone by
If I was good and strong
An ornate gate was waiting
Though the road be hard and long
The end result would depend
On how I worked and played
But no one told me how or what

'Your own rules must be obeyed'

What shall I find eventually?

'Everyone must reach the gate'

After travelling long, with effort
Will I, then, be told to wait?
Will I find a gold keyhole
Locked from the other side?
Or fierce dogs guarding
And nowhere for me to hide?
Will there be a janitor who
Ignores my desperate plea?
Or will I be told that through
That gate I will never be?

Is there more that I must do?
Well if so, then I don't know
I will just call for someone else
My weariness must show
To someone with eyes to see
And ears that hear my cry
I will ask to have some help
As I can no longer try
I have been thinking and decided
I shall say

'I've done my best
And if it's not been good enough
Then, please
Accept me as a guest'

I shall request to stay a while
To have some food and sleep
Then I can be sent away
If my room I cannot keep
It matters very little now
I have neither hope nor fears
I will journey where I can
Till another gate appears

I shall ask,

'Do the mighty in the land
Enter any gate with ease?
Or the heads of religious sects
Do they the guardians please?'

'It is not the position or beliefs
That determines each man's fate
But the way they chose to travel
To the waiting ornate gate'

The Question

'What is life?'

So many ask
This journey we all take
Is it a path already laid?
Or one that we must make
We didn't ask to be born
As far as we can tell
Life can be like heaven
Other times resembles hell
Do we travel through each day?
Follow where integrity leads?
Divert for another's approval?
Or to just to satisfy our needs?
Do we seek only pleasure?
Or stray from what is right?
That way we can easily turn
Our daytime into night
Or can we battle for the truth?
What is life's pain - endure
Fight the cause and travel on
Our choice
That is for sure

▶ ◀

The Reckoning

Where no mercy is given
None shall be received
Your reckoning will come
Do not be deceived
Religion won't save you
Actions are all recorded
In your mind they remain
And no ransom afforded

Evil leaves a dark cloud
Hanging over our lands
Created by ugly minds and
Carried out with fearful hands
Hell awaits, and in that place
The pain inflicted shall return
To live with them for ever
Those fires will always burn

<u>The Same</u>

If I had been given a choice to be
Would I have been born as me?

Had I known the painful road
Would I have picked the same abode?

Through the Valley of Death I've been
I can relate what I have seen

At the Gate of Heaven a voice I heard
I can remember every word

But still I travel with hope, and yet
Despite the pain I have no regret

I would go through it all, and even more
For you to arrive at my front door

The Solution

The man was very funny as he raced up and down

'Who are you?'

Someone said

'Oh! Me? I'm just a clown
I like to make people laugh and I try to bring some joy
I want to bring a smile to every girl and boy'

The man was very sad as he walked slowly by

'Who are you?'

Someone said

'Someone trying not to cry
For all the little children who never have a smile
I am going round the world. I have walked for many a mile'

The man looked very old
As he rode his donkey past

'How are you?'

Someone said

'I feel kindness here, at last
I have travelled everywhere and have seen so many places
I am searching to see happiness on all the children's faces
Then I shall know I have found where the answer lies
If children are happy a future can realise

Wars will not happen and all fighting cease
When all our children grow to be adults seeking peace'

▶◀

The Sting of Death

Where is the sting of death?
I know not of its being
Where I went was beautiful
The sting was in the living
Coming back to endless pain
No release, no joy to be
Anger felt at the injustice
There was no place for me

I want to live, not exist, with
Freedom to breath and talk
No straightjacket of ill lungs
Immobile, so I cannot walk
When I am well, can live again
I hope to forget this past
But the sting was very painful
Its effects just seem to last

When pain has gone I shall rejoice
That 'my table' was not set
I want to be with those I love
I have much work - as yet
Not many know the feeling
Of rejection from on high
Please avoid it, if you can
It would make the strongest cry

▶ ◀

The Switch

I have a deep and hidden switch
Hidden somewhere in my head
I don't know how to reach it
It unconsciously works instead
When the switch, for care and love
Allows strong power to flow
There is energy in abundance and
The ones who receive it know

But, when the switch is turned off
The wires are disconnected
For no matter what happens after
From all hurt I am protected
As though a very long fuse wire
To a flame has been directed
When it burns the required length
Then the system is perfected

So, should someone I love give
Prolonged anger, hurt or pain
Something happens gradually
In that area of my brain
Behaviour to them will not change
Though my eyes may both look cold
I shall do what I do from kindness
Not from love, as was of old

This is something beyond my power
But the result I do not waste
I can care deeply and for long
I do not lose that love in haste
But once switched 'off', no circuit left
No resentment do I feel
It is as if that love never was
In that way my heart can heal

►◄

The Taj Mahal

One beautiful, amazing building
Built by hands and sweat and tears
White with dazzling jewels
Evidence of many workers' years
Truly magnificent, with great splendour
High above a river, flowing, wide
Small windows restrict the light
From the ornate tomb inside

It was built in deep mourning
When a wealthy man's wife died
He built it, 'a symbol of his love'
Her last labour was not survived
But was it love? I would ask you
Is a fourteenth child 'a must'?
Or did guilt build the temple
A monument to carnal lust?

Had he truly loved his wife
He would, surely, have used his head
Realised the obvious dangers
But he used his loins instead
Had his heart been really true
(I am not trying to be funny)
But he would have valued her life
And also saved a lot of money

There is an epilogue to relate
This loving, grieving man - so kind
Gave the architect a parting gift
(Apparently, so we were told)
Both eyes were rendered blind
So he could not repeat the triumph
No other similar creations make
But were these also the actions
That any good man would take?

The Truth about Religion

What do religious leaders know
Of heaven, but out of books?
Studied to give them answers
Behind the words, still no one looks
No God appoints them to the task
No calling, but deep desire
To be among the chosen few
To avoid the flames of eternal fire

But it doesn't work like that
Belief does not a ticket buy
To go through the gate of heaven
More than that men need to try
Selfish dogma, powerful words
Dressed in uniform and robe
Have no power to deliver
Or the spirit realms to probe

Behind religion, Satan works
In heaven he plans to rule
To conquer by the fear of hell
Using the ministries as his tool
Different religions fuel the fire
Behind most wars and fight
Causing pain to great extent
Blocking many people's light

They have no right to brainwash
To hold people in their thrall
Retribution will be for those
And many from heights will fall
Religion is not serving God
He asks not that men should kneel
But to show care and kindness
And another's needs to feel

►◄

The Unrelenting Storm

I am broken
Torn part
By wind and tempest
Rushing storm

No shelter
Or refuge found
Against the force
I have no form

Ice cuts through
My heart is dead
No feeling left
Gone with pain

Without ending
Torment fierce
Do I fall to never
Live again?

~

No!

I shall survive
Have days to meet

The storm ends
My body mends

▶ ◀

The Vigil

My time is for waiting
Again to hear your voice
Gone, just in a flicker
Of eyelid, without choice
No preparation given
No plans that we could share
Gone, before I knew it
I looked, you were not there
Alone I faced the perils
The sea of life to cross
Always waiting patiently
Remembering your loss
Battered by the storms
That almost broke my mast
Lost in the fog of pain
Thinking to breathe my last
Somewhere, on an island
Under myriad stars of night
I wait to hear your call
Let darkness turn to light
Can you still remember
My name through all the years?
I still cannot think of yours
Without crying many tears
Always waiting patiently
I dare not go to sleep
Just in case I miss your call
My silent vigil keep
Do not shout. I'm listening
Just whisper. I shall hear
No more endless isolation
Banished will be all fear
But, until then I survive
I carry on, I do my best
I live my years, as do others
One day you'll know the rest

▶ ◀

The Visitors

When she was young and very ill
Awake in pain all night
Two ladies used to visit
Bringing comfort and a light
Sometimes they would sing
Sometimes would read a book
One used to hold her hand
The other would stand and look

They wore different clothes
From the women round about
They were small, their dresses long
Softly spoken, they did not shout
Where they came from, who can say?
They were there, just by her bed
They didn't come in through the door
Maybe through the wall instead

One night they did not arrive
Though she was in great pain
She did not know the reason
Sadly, they never came again
She decided to write a letter
And put it on her shelf
She was six, could only print
But she did it all herself

'Dear Kind Ladies

You have left and gone away
I try but cannot see
I want to say thank you
For coming to be with me
I never had the chance
To thank you face to face

So I am leaving this letter
In an open, empty place
I may be asleep and hope
You see it with your light
I shall never forget you
Love to you both
Goodnight'

Just when she needed help
It came in that strange way
Since then she believes in angels
That experience will always stay
Maybe they became too busy
Or they had to spread their joy

I like to think they went to comfort
Another small girl or boy

The Way of the Ungodly

Cloaked in the finest garments
Of silks, satin, ermine, gold
Evil walks upon the world
Gathering many unto its fold
Hidden in dogma and beliefs
People's minds within its thrall
Creating a world of 'no questioning'
Spreading news 'hell waits for all'

Harboured in the minds of men
The scythe of suffering wields
But those who really understand
Never to its power yields
Terror, devastation, pain
Fuel hell's eternal fire
The power of religion over minds
Is sinister and more dire

Undetected, it roams the world
Mocking the foolishness around
Men searching in selfish ways
Their own salvation to be found
Pretending with manmade rules
All religions subjugate
Anyone who is good and kind
Has credence at the final gate

Wars and pain in whatever name
Around the world, in every land
Allow evil to spread dark wings
Decide!
On whose side do you stand?
In the spirit world, all are known
No hiding, the truth must face
Only kind behaviour on this earth
Leads to an eternal resting place

▶ ◀

The Window

The window overlooked some trees
Far above - a cloudless sky
Laughter echoed through the light
But all she could do was cry
She looked out to see the world
How she longed to be a part
But an inner wall was between
The pain just broke her heart

From illness with its rejections
Freedom, never near her door
While she wished to participate
Others simply asked for more
Drained with isolation's fears
None to seek, she was alone
Wrapped in a black mantle
Then she heard a distant moan

'Who can feel such awful anguish?'

She wondered but couldn't see
Then quite suddenly she realised

'That noise must come from me
If only the pain would vanish
I could start my life anew
Then all would be so different
As I dance on morning dew
I would climb a highest mountain
Swim with dolphins in the sea
My dreams must keep me going
One day they will come to be
Until then I shall make no fuss
Nor listen to inner strife
Wait with patience and hope to see
A window opening in my life'

▶ ◀

Things That Cannot Be Bought

I saw a man. He had a coat, like gold it shone so clear
I asked him where he bought it and had it cost him dear?

'You cannot buy a coat like this'

He replied to me

'It is called Courage, but it did not come free
'I went through a field of pain. I reached the other side
I had no one to help me and no horse with me to ride'

I saw a man with a hat. It was like a silver moon
I asked him where he bought it and could I get one soon?

'You cannot buy a hat like this'

He replied to me

'It is called Kindness and it did not come free
I helped one who was lost and one who could not walk
One who had no food and drink and one too ill to talk'

I saw a man with shiny boots, strong, light as a feather
I asked him where he bought them. He said he hadn't - ever

'You cannot buy boots like these'

He replied to me

'They are called Endurance and they do not come free
I had to work beyond my strength and for so very long
No other there to lift the load and no help came along'

I saw a man with a light that shone so far and bright
I asked him where he bought it as it beamed into the night

'You cannot buy a light like this'

He replied to me

'It is called eternal Hope it was given to me - free
I had lost direction
I had battled to the end
I had coped when all seemed lost. For myself I had to fend

Then a light I suddenly saw upon my darkest day
I did not ask.
It was just there. And then I found my way'

You have to find your Courage
Kindness comes from very deep
Endurance needs much effort

But

Hope is yours to keep

▶ ◀

This Time

Am I modern? Hard to say
I like computers, the life today
Light and heat, cars to travel
Still a lot I must unravel

Things I hate, loud music blaring
Selfishness and much uncaring
Children left for endless hours
Away from home, with no powers

Money wasted in excess
Some 'nouveau riche' caring less
Women's clothes bare midriffs show
Cold ignored when east winds blow

Needless fighting, religion's hand
Stealing other people's land
Obsession with 'celebrity' life
Children's pain in times of strife

'Over the top' outlays of grief
The families then get no relief
I could go on and weary make
Does anyone any notice take?

The future lies with the children
But what messages are they getting?
Money, selfishness, drink and drugs
Important things - we are forgetting

Time for Tears

How empty is this place
You were, but are no more
Someone took you by the hand
And led you through the door
Away from your earthly life
To live on a different plane
It means that our days here
Will never be quite the same

From the bond that bound us
You are now free to roam
Gone to a much better place
To a very different home
I hope that where you now abide
We are in your thoughts some day
And maybe when the time arrives
You'll welcome us to stay

Till then your memory lingers
Pictures, sounds of hours spent
Serious concern, much laughter
Time together quickly went
Latterly we could only sit
When your body felt the years
I shared much of your life
Now
An empty chair holds many tears

Time to 'Pay Back'

You are glad that I survived

But

To get through to the end
So you can still hold my hand
Though you never asked me
Love gave me my command

'Leave not in your despair
In pain that will not ease
Please, keep going to the end
Until your trials cease
Never underestimate
Pain's strength or power'

I was not allowed to die
Clinging on from hour by hour
My love would not let me
Leave, 'call it a day'
But for all my effort
There is a price to pay

Work to be fit and healthy
From you I ask no more
I could easily have decided
To enter the waiting door
Your own deserve the same
Effort - true and strong
Your love for them will help
Even if the way seems long

You owe me nothing
But for them I would cry
Do the best, as I have done
Understand the reason why

Pay back time comes to all
Whether good or bad
Love makes its own demands
But only to make you glad

Simple care of yourself
Whatever work demands
Could ensure you are around
To hold your children's hands

To a New Baby

When you arrived to be with us
And safe journey had been made
Your eyes slowly opened wide
You saw smiles that will not fade

Warmth now surrounds you
Of love both pure and deep
That promise we can give you
A timeless gift for you to keep

What life holds we cannot tell
No one can your future know
But
Surrounded by such devotion
Your little self can safely grow

Sheltered by love from all storms
May your ship sail waters calm
And angels guide your life's path
And protect you from all harm

May your feet dance your steps
Through life let your voice sing
So the world will hear and love
The message that you bring

A gift of innocence and truth
A babe is born with naught
Except the key to doors of love
That most truly, you have brought

▶ ◀

Together

Together we have faced the storm
Waiting for new day to dawn

Together walked the rocky way
Hoping for the end of day

Together faced the grief and pain
Holding hands, strength to gain

Together, through the endless strife
To reach the meaning of our life

Together, a word that means so much
From laughter to a gentle touch

With each other, we'll reach the end
Harmony and Love, together blend

Too Busy

Have I ever been too busy for your needs?
I have to wonder
Has what I have had to do been more important?
I now ponder
I cannot at this moment think of a time when that was true
But, I do understand it may have seemed like that to you

Were there times in your life when your needs
I ignored,
Was I not there to comfort you when
An inner panic soared?
If so, I am sorry, as you were always top of my list
But, I may not have listened and something would be missed

Realise, that I too had times when I needed a helping hand
Or listening ear
Not often, you understand, but there
Nevertheless, I fear
So, just a phone call, an occasional visit to see
Is all I want, without request, just for me and given free

▶ ◀

Too Late to Cry

Years change, unfamiliar
Feelings will be shown
As the children leave the nest
And venture in realms unknown

'Take your mobile. Let us know
How you're getting on
Answer any letters
Don't let any day be gone
Without contact. We need
To know that you are fine'

A first time caring parents
Walk along the fragile line
Between natural concern and protection
While hiding many fears
As teenagers finally leave home
They try to stop the anxious tears

'I'll be OK, it's really cool. I just can't wait to go'

'Take good care. That's all we ask'

Is said, the mood sinks low

'Have we done enough to prepare him/her for the fray?'

'We tried our best. That's all that we can say'

'Please God it all works out OK'

The inner voice now speaks
The car drives off, and finally
Only sadness their company keeps

Never again will it be
The same 'nest' as before

Acceptance is a challenge
Past time returns no more

Make the best of those years
So there will be no regret
Waiting to cause havoc
As you cannot forget
The times that you wasted
The hours you were not there
Or the opportunities missed
When your child needed care

The goodnight hugs and kisses
You were not there to give
As work was more important or
The way you chose to live
The bruise or scratch or cut
Comforted in your stead?
Or maybe, even, times ignored
Their needs not in your head

Often when faced with certainty
Past decisions seem awry
But, remember this proverb

'A time can be too late to cry'

Will it be? Can you prepare?
Do you understand the need?

'Continued care through those years'

This simple message all should heed

▶◀

Transfixed

The pain was like a spiral of
Barbed wire. It would not ease
About the chest. She could not breathe
And could find no ease
No way was there to loosen
The hold was sharp and tight
She knew she could not break out
Had no effort left to fight
All human resources used to cope
Nothing remained in any store
All drained away eventually
No where to find some more

But there was no-one near
None a rescue made
Her fate was sealed and finished
Goodbye to that young maid
Cruelty was part of that time
But is it different in this age?
In generations yet to come
Will someone write this page?
Something learned of nothing gained?
Any change that now survives?
Not while
The belief in 'wars and fight'
Governs the few who rule our lives

►◄

Tribute to my Mother

If you couldn't see to find your way
Your map of life had gone
You were old, lost, and frail
And dependent days were long
Would you moan and loudly groan
Your anguish for all to hear?
Or endure, with patience and a smile
Sometimes shed a silent tear?

An inspiration to those who cared
Her final year became
When beliefs and true normality
Could never be the same
Adapting bravely to all change
The only outcome was 'the end'
Relying on others totally
For herself she could not fend

She walked that path with dignity
Courage shown in every way
Resolute till her latest hour
Still wanting to meet each day
She showed a touching compassion
For others frail and weak
Yet, she did not bemoan herself
No sympathy did she seek

We cannot know what is in store
As we choose our paths in life
We may meet, through no fault
Many trials, illness, strife
But if choice is lost, would that we
Show inner beauty such as she
Accepting, with grace and serenity
What was and what had to be

▶ ◀

Unselfish Love

I needed to understand
To wait patiently, with hope
I needed a companion
To listen and help me cope
I needed care when in pain
Someone to hold my hand
I needed food to be brought
When too ill to stand

I needed to be cared for
Against my wishes I was ill
And you were there besides me
And you truly love me still
Despite the fact I did nothing
Lay in bed from morn till night
You continued your selfless love
While I against pain did fight

We shall walk together again
Visit places we don't know
And have years of joy ahead
When my health begins to flow
I am certain this will happen
I believe illness will be gone
I thank you for the love and care
Which made me carry on

Waste Not Time

Is this how I must live?
Away from faces new
Looking from the window
See for ever the same view?

Is this what I must accept?
Live in a house of pain
Never more to travel
Feel the warmth of sun again?

Is this the end of endeavour?
Is there no more I can do?
Can I not find another door?
And the key to let me through?

Is my effort not enough?
No sacrifice too great?
There is no answer in the sky
I shall just have to wait

If this is how I must live
I accept but not by choice
In another way I shall be heard
Though no one hears my voice

But I can think and I can write
And on pages a story tell
Of how the good conquered all
And sent the bad to hell

► ◄

Where is The Way?

Is that the way to happiness?
Can you teach me not to care?
Not to feel another's need?
Or another's anguish share?
Can you show me how it's done?
I'd really like to know
As others seem to get on well
When concern they do not show

Is that the way to happiness?
To avoid the children's eyes?
To see beyond the misery
Caused by hunger, shouts or lies?
How do people jump for joy?
When music is so loud
Am I missing something here?
Am I wrapped in endless shroud?

Is that the way to happiness?
If so, then count me out
I cannot drug my mind away
Block the world in drinking bout
To be loved is all I need or want
My soul-mate to walk with me
To seek happiness is irrelevant
What will be is what will be

Then I can face all the pain
I can tolerate the fears
I can reason away the anger
Release the burning tears
A strength born out of courage
Will be sustained by love
And happiness will be waiting
In the spiritual halls above

► ◄

What is Life About?

A life that's lived for pleasure
What rewards does it bring?
It stimulates the senses but
Does it make your heart sing?

What is the purpose of our lives?
What do we leave behind?
Do we vanish as if never been?
Or will someone a relic find?

It is not about status or possessions
It is not about position or wealth
It is not about going to church
It is about how we conduct ourselves

It is about our honesty and kindness
About good values within us deep
It is about caring for each other
And having standards that we keep

The ones who organise bloodshed
Will not escape their fate
The terrorists will not find heaven
They will be driven to hell by hate

Each one must make life's journey
Why chose a boat that has a leak?
Some are so wrecked and damaged
That afloat they cannot keep

Life is to be lived we all know
That is the purpose clear
But to be kind and to give love
Those achievements I hold dear

▶ ◀

When All Have Left

I've used my mental energy
And all my inner strength
And travelled with endurance
Valued patience at great length
Hope accompanied my footsteps
Enthusiasm gave the light
But now all have departed
It seems as dark as night
The courage that sustained me
Has melted as the snow
No stars shine in the present
Future direction I don't know
How can I tread the final path?
If more pain I have to meet
I fear what may be hidden
In the days still left to greet
I was given a promise

'You will never have to face
More pain than you can bear
In any time or any place'

But someone has forgotten
Those words that I was told
And now I am exhausted, tired
As pain has made me old

Who Will Look After You?

Who will look after you
When you are unwell?
As that fate is certain
In truth, I can tell
If you continue
Your lifestyle to live
Then only yourself
Will you have to forgive

Your diet of alcohol
Drunk in excess
Will damage your liver
Or more - nothing less
Sickness and nausea
All the day through
Itching incessantly
In store for you

Cannabis, dope
Call it by any name
To the brain can be dire
The effects all the same
Being paranoid ruins
Friendships and life
Schizophrenia brings
Just dreadful strife

Unless you prepare
No one will be there
With skills to help
Your pain to bear
By then, we shall all
Have died and gone
But yet your damage
Will have been done

Your choice, your life
Who am I to say
What you should do?
All must choose their way
But just take a moment
Give yourself a clear view
Twenty years have passed
Who looks after you?

Why Was I Born?

Why was I born when no one has love for me all day?
What purpose? What decision? What game does someone play?
I am not an adult. My day, another chooses
But when I do not feel love
I am the one who loses

I shall learn not to care. I shall not even cry
I shall look quite happy, and never have to try
But, I am not an adult. I have no rights. I cannot talk
No one will ever know
The path I have to walk

I will ask a question. Were you alone and sad?
Left with strangers when very young? Yet had done nothing bad?
Though I am not an adult, I know just what I need
It seems that no one cares enough
And neither do you heed

What will I do I wonder? I cannot my anguish say
Maybe to love is hard work, but there is no other way
An adult's life is expensive, but love cannot be bought
How shall I learn how to live?
When I came here with naught?

Would it be different if I had brought jewels, money, wealth?
Would you love me then or just offer 'food for health'?
Which adult can I ask when no answers I can gain?
I want to be loved, but instead all I feel
Is a deep and awful, nagging pain?

▶ ◀

Without Mercy

I, too, can look and not see
Some who wait in front of me
When Mercy died at evil's hand
In her place no one could stand
For those who hurt with intent
This message has, for you, been sent

'Whom you meet, you may not know
Until at the final gate you show
Then the time will be too late
You may change, but not your fate
That weak child, with dreadful fear
Who you hurt, no one could hear
The tree of eternal life now shades
But her memory never fades
Her silent witness, no words said
Understand - all deeds are read'

Evil actions will all endure
Like a boomerang flying sure
They return back to the doer
Hell awaits - the final sewer
No power in heaven or on earth
Can alter an act once given birth
They may be good, they may be bad
Think and learn! You will be glad

Mercy cares for children, small
Hurt just one, you hurt them all
If she sees you as you walk
She will never with you talk
Lies to her you can not tell
Your place awaits. It is in hell
What you do, you cannot hide
The truth is known once you have died

► ◄